OCEANS

LOOKING AT BEACHES AND CORAL REEFS,

TIDES AND CURRENTS,

SEA MAMMALS AND FISH,

SEAWEEDS

AND OTHER OCEAN WONDERS

Kids Can Press Ltd. acknowledges with appreciation the assistance of the Canada Council and the Ontario Arts Council in the production of this book.

Canadian Cataloguing in Publication Data

Mason, Adrienne
    Oceans : looking at beaches and coral reefs, tides and currents, sea mammals and fish, seaweeds and other ocean wonders

Includes index
ISBN 1-55074-147-0

1. Marine biology – Juvenile literature. 2. Oceans – Juvenile literature. I. Gatt, Elizabeth, 1951– II. Title.

QH91.16.M38 1995   j574.92   C94-932768-9

Kids Can Press Ltd.
29 Birch Avenue
Toronto, Ontario, Canada
M4V 1E2

Edited by Valerie Wyatt
Designed by Arifin A. Graham, Alaris Design
Cover design by Marie Bartholomew
Printed and bound in Hong Kong

95 0 9 8 7 6 5 4 3 2 1

OCEANS

LOOKING AT BEACHES AND CORAL REEFS, TIDES AND CURRENTS, SEA MAMMALS AND FISH, SEAWEEDS AND OTHER OCEAN WONDERS

WRITTEN BY
ADRIENNE MASON

ILLUSTRATIONS BY
ELIZABETH GATT

PHOTOGRAPHS BY
DAVID DENNING

ST. PAUL'S SCHOOL
PETERBOROUGH

KIDS CAN PRESS LTD
TORONTO

For my parents, who had the good sense to raise me by the sea.

Acknowledgements

Many people have provided invaluable assistance with this book but none more than my editor, Valerie Wyatt, who led me through this seemingly endless project with confidence and a great sense of humour. I would also like to thank the many scientists who checked the accuracy of the manuscript: Dr. Bill Austin, Khoyatan Marine Lab; Dr. Joe Buckley, Department of Physics, Royal Roads Military College; Dr. Louis Druehl, Bamfield Marine Station; David Denning; Dr. John Ford, Vancouver Public Aquarium; Dr. Mark Graham, Vancouver Public Aquarium; Phil Lambert, Royal B.C. Museum; Dr. André Martel, Canadian Museum of Nature; Dr. Dawn Renfrew, Bamfield Marine Station; Dr. Nancy Sanders, Northeast Missouri State University; James Steel, Huntsman Marine Science Centre; and Dr. Verena Tunnicliffe, University of Victoria. Judy Ashurst and the grade five and six students and teachers at Willows School in Victoria, B.C., enthusiastically field-tested the activities and made valuable suggestions. Emma and Stephen Buckley voluntarily read through parts of the manuscript to test that complex scientific material was "kid-friendly." Thank you all. Finally, I would like to thank my husband, Bob Hansen, who constantly provides encouragement and support for all of my endeavours.

Contents

The ocean as home

Have you ever wondered about the ocean? Why is it salty? How deep is it? Where do waves come from? How do animals survive in such salty water? If you're curious about the ocean and the creatures that live in it, this book is for you. Read about animals that live between grains of sand (page 23)

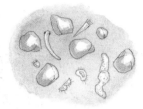

or sharks that have 20 rows of teeth (page 52).

Turn your fish dinner into a picture for your wall (page 50) or make some waves (page 13).

Find out about life on the ocean bottom (page 65)

and underwater forests (page 40).

You don't need any special equipment to explore the oceans. You don't even need to live near the ocean. Just curl up somewhere warm and dry and turn the page. Your ocean adventure is about to begin ...

Your devotion to the ocean

Even if you live inland, the ocean is important to you:
- *because many of Earth's weather patterns are shaped by the ocean*
- *because the air you breathe was created by life in the sea*
- *because many of the things you use are transported to you on the ocean*
- *because many of the foods you eat come from the sea*
- *because life on Earth had its beginnings in the ocean.*

The blue planet

Look at this picture of Earth taken from space. Notice how blue it looks? Earth looks blue because ocean covers 71 per cent of it. Perhaps Earth should have been called Ocean instead!

Next time you eat an apple, cut it into four pieces first. If one quarter represents the amount of land on Earth, the other three quarters represent Earth's water (both salt and fresh water). Of those remaining three quarters of the apple, only a tiny sliver (about 3 per cent) is fresh water. The rest is salt water, and most of it is in the oceans.

There are four major oceans in the world: the Pacific, Atlantic, Indian and Arctic. Which ocean is closest to you? On a globe or world map, see if you can trace a route from one ocean to another. Surprised? Even though the world's oceans have different names, they are all connected to form one huge ocean.

Life in the ocean is very different from life on land. Most of the ocean is salty, dark, deep and cold, not really a place you would choose to live. Yet the oceans are home to a wide variety of life, from tiny bacteria, much smaller than the dot on this "i," to the largest animal in the world, the blue whale.

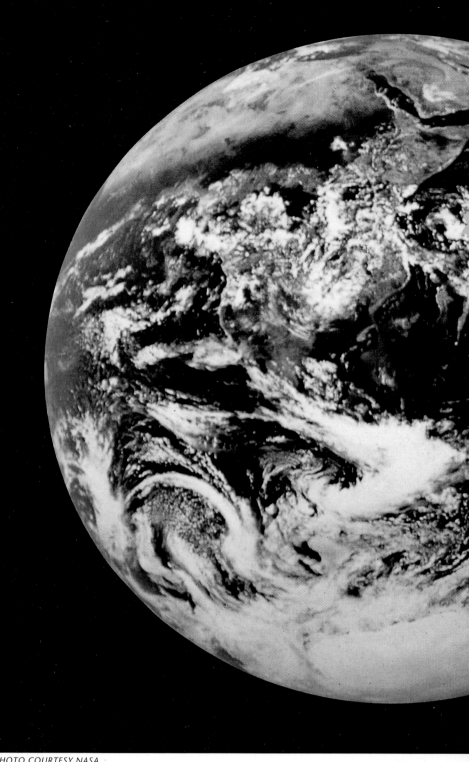

PHOTO COURTESY NASA

How salty is the ocean?

If all of the salt were removed from the ocean and spread evenly over the land, it would form a layer more than 152 m (500 feet) thick – deep enough to cover a 40-storey building!

Ocean gold rush

The ocean is full of tiny particles of gold – about $22 000 000 worth of gold in a km^3 ($93 000 000 in a cubic mile) of sea water. Unfortunately, because the gold particles are so tiny, ocean gold is very difficult to retrieve.

Salt of the ocean

If you left a pail of ocean water out in the sun, the water would evaporate and you'd find a crust of salt on the bottom of your pail. Many countries get the salt they need this way – by flooding shallow areas with sea water and letting the water evaporate.

The salt in the oceans is similar to the salt you put on your food. It is mostly sodium chloride, with a sprinkling of other salts including magnesium, sulphur, calcium and potassium. It even has bits of minerals such as gold and arsenic. All of these salts and minerals are vital for life in the sea.

How does salt get into the sea? Most sea salt comes from the land. As water flows over the land and in rivers, it dissolves salts from soil and rock and eventually carries them to the sea. Some of the salts also come from underwater volcanoes and places deep in the sea floor where hot magma bubbles up from the centre of the Earth.

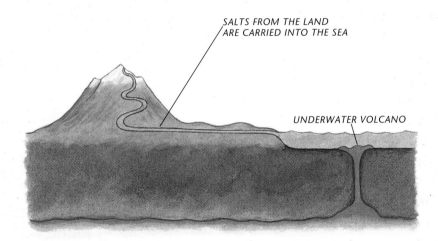

SALTS FROM THE LAND ARE CARRIED INTO THE SEA

UNDERWATER VOLCANO

Salts are also taken out of the ocean. Salts in sea spray are carried into the air as passengers on tiny water droplets. Other salts are taken out of the ocean by sea plants and animals. Shells, for example, are made from the salts of calcium.

The saltiness, or "salinity," of sea water varies throughout the oceans. On average, there are 35 parts of salt for every 1000 parts of water. This means that for every 1000 kg (or pounds) of sea water, 35 kg (or pounds) are salt. The saltiest ocean in the world is the Red Sea. There the salt content is over 40 parts per thousand (ppt). Deep in the Red Sea are places where supersalty water bubbles up through cracks in the sea floor. Here the salt content is 257 ppt! Drinking this water would be like drinking 250 mL (1 cup) of water with 60 mL (4 tablespoons) of salt in it. Average sea water would only have 9 mL (2 teaspoons) salt in 250 mL (1 cup). Still pretty salty!

This sea snail took salts from the ocean to make its shell.

Water, water, everywhere...

Q: If you were shipwrecked, could you survive by drinking sea water?
A: No. Sea water would actually dry you out – you would become "dehydrated." Why? You carry a sea within you – salty body fluids. (Don't believe it? Just lick your hand after you've been sweating for a while.) Salts are important for muscle contractions (including your heartbeat), digestion and proper functioning of nerves.

If you drank sea water you'd have too much salt. Your body would try to get rid of the extra salt, to get back to normal. The only way to do that would be to drink lots of fresh water, which would dilute the salt. Then you could urinate more and flush out the salt. If no fresh water was available, you'd be in trouble. Your body would start to steal precious water from other places such as your cells and blood. You'd lose water and become dehydrated. That would make you very sick.

But take heart. If you were unlucky enough to be shipwrecked, you could make fresh water from salt water. Try "Make a Freshwater Still," next page.

Your body contains about 250 g (8.8 ounces) of salt.

Make a freshwater still

The word "still" comes from "distillation," which means extracting a liquid, drop by drop, from another liquid. This still will allow you to distill fresh water.

You'll need:
salt water – stir 30 mL (2 tbsp) of salt into 1L (4 cups)
   of water
a large, dark-coloured bowl
a drinking glass
clean stones
plastic wrap
masking tape

1. Pour some salt water into the bowl to a depth of 7.5 cm (3 inches).

2. Place the glass, right side up, in the centre of the bowl. If the glass starts to float, anchor it with some clean stones.

3. Cover the bowl with plastic wrap, securing it around the rim with masking tape. Put a stone in the centre of the plastic wrap directly over the centre of the glass as shown. The plastic wrap will sag downward over the glass.

4. Place your still in a sunny area or under a lamp.

The water in the salt water evaporates and condenses on the plastic wrap. This water drips into the glass. Taste the water. Is it salty? When the water evaporates, the salt is left behind.

Nature's still

In nature, the sun turns tonnes (tons) of sea water into fresh water every day. This is how much of the world's rainwater is produced.

The sun beams down on the ocean, causing water to evaporate. The water vapour forms clouds and rain falls.

The ocean in motion

The ocean is always in motion. Waves roll over the sea surface. Major ocean currents flow like rivers. And tides rise and fall. What causes all that churning, crashing and surging?

WAVES

Waves are caused by the wind blowing over the ocean surface. Waves can vary in height from tiny ripples to storm waves more than 30 m (98 feet) tall. The size of waves depends on the speed of the wind (velocity), the length of time the wind blows (duration) and the distance over which it blows (fetch). A light breeze blowing for a short time and distance will make gentle waves. But a big blow over a long time and distance will give you crashing waves that would make even a surfer shudder.

The biggest waves are tsunamis. Although they are often called tidal waves, tsunamis aren't actually caused by tides. Earthquakes, volcanic eruptions and underwater landslides cause these monster waves.

When you watch waves, it looks as if the water is moving forward. But is it really? Watch birds or logs bobbing on the water's surface. They don't move forward with every wave that passes under them. They just bob up and down. Try "Rub-a-dub Ducky" and see for yourself.

The water droplets in a wave don't actually move forward. They move in a small circle. Only the energy of the wave travels forward. With waves close to shore, the bottom of the wave drags on the ocean bottom and slows down. The crest (top) of the wave keeps moving, though, and the wave "breaks" on the beach.

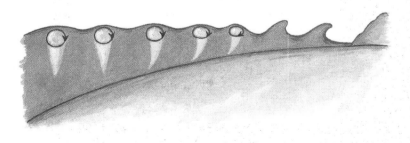

Rub-a-dub ducky

You'll need:
a rubber duck or something else that
will float

1. Float the duck (or other object)
   in the middle of a bathtub.

2. Make waves at one end of the
   tub by holding your hand just
   below the surface and moving
   it gently up and down in a
   steady motion. Try to generate
   slow, steady waves. Does the
   duck move forward or stay in
   one spot?

CURRENTS: RIVERS IN THE SEA

On May 27, 1990, the ship *Hansa Carrier* encountered a severe storm in the north Pacific Ocean. Twenty-one shipping containers were lost overboard. Five of these containers held 80 000 pairs of Nike shoes, ranging from children's runners to men's hiking boots.

To the delight of beachcombers, shoes soon started washing up on beaches from the Queen Charlotte Islands to southern Oregon. Some shoes even beached in Hawaii! The shoes weren't tied together, so it was difficult to find matching pairs. Avid beachcombers solved this problem by holding swapmeets.

The shoes took a ride on the "rivers in the sea" – ocean currents – which circulate ocean water all over the world. There are two major types of ocean currents: surface currents and deep-water currents.

Surface currents are caused by the Earth's prevailing winds (steady winds that blow continuously in one direction). As these winds blow, they push the water on the ocean's surface.

Deep-water currents are responsible for circulating ocean water around the world. Differences in the salinity (saltiness) of water can cause deep-water currents. In warm climates, such as the Mediterranean, water evaporates from the surface of the ocean. This makes the remaining surface water extra salty. This high-salt water sinks and mixes with the water at lower depths, taking much-needed oxygen down with it. See how salt water sinks in Experiment 1 on the next page.

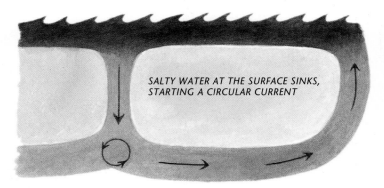

SALTY WATER AT THE SURFACE SINKS, STARTING A CIRCULAR CURRENT

Other deep-water currents occur when cold water at the poles sinks and slowly moves towards the equator. Warm deep-water currents travel from the equator to the poles to replace the sinking cold water. Experiment with sinking cold water in Experiment 2 on the next page.

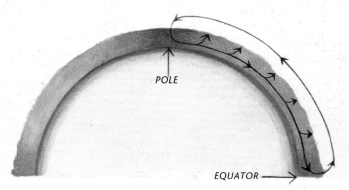

POLE

EQUATOR

Create some ocean currents

You'll need:
2 drinking glasses
salt
measuring spoons
food colouring
a teaspoon
an ice-cube tray
a glass cake pan or baking dish

Experiment #1

1. Half-fill the glasses with tap water. Stir 10 mL (2 tsp) of salt into one of the glasses and add 4 or 5 drops of food colouring so that you can tell the salt water from the fresh. Stir well.
2. Using the teaspoon, slowly pour some of the coloured salt water onto the surface of the fresh water. What happens?

The salt water sinks because it is denser, or heavier, than the fresh water. The same thing happens in the ocean, creating currents.

Cold water is also heavier than warm water. Don't believe it? Try the next experiment.

Experiment #2

1. Fill two ice-cube moulds with tap water. Add a drop of food colouring to each mould. Freeze the water.
2. Fill a glass cake pan or baking dish with lukewarm water.
3. Place the two coloured ice cubes at one end of the pan or dish. What happens?

Cold water is denser than warm water. Denser, cold water sinks and less dense warm water rises. So as the ice cubes begin to melt, the cold water sinks to the bottom. This is what starts some deep-water currents in the oceans.

These By-the-wind sailors were carried by the currents and beached by blowing winds.

Deep-water currents carry much-needed oxygen from the surface down to the ocean's depths. And they bring nutrients (food) up to the surface. Places where nutrients are brought to the surface by deep-water currents are called "areas of upwelling." Fish are attracted by the food, so these areas are often good fishing grounds.

Ocean currents circulate the oceans' water. They also affect the climate on the land nearby. Warm currents such as the Atlantic's Gulf Stream bring warmer temperatures to areas that would otherwise be much colder. The Gulf Stream flows from the Gulf of Mexico past the east coast of the United States and over to northern Europe. If it weren't for the Gulf Stream, people in England would need snowshoes and winter boots instead of umbrellas and raincoats. Look on the map below. Is there a major ocean current near your home?

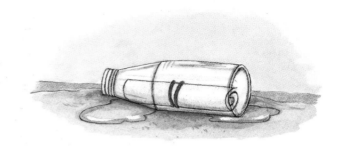

Ocean mail

Dorothy Dalba was visiting the west coast of Vancouver Island when she noticed a bottle lying on the beach. She opened the bottle and found a message from a student in Japan.

It took more than three years for the ocean currents to deliver the message 6000 km (3728 miles). Talk about a slow, but special, delivery! Check the map below to see which currents might have delivered the message.

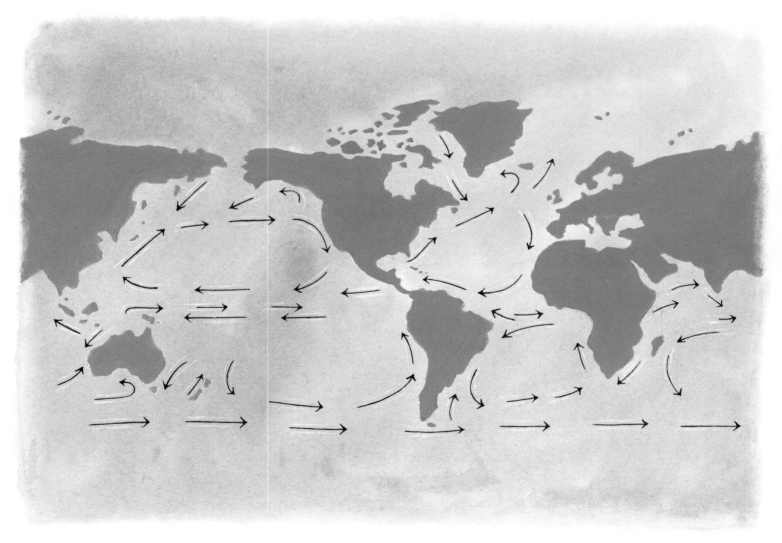

TIDES

Susannah and Peter are visiting the seashore and decide to build a sandcastle. They choose a nice flat spot near the water's edge. After working for an hour they get hungry and run off to find their parents and their picnic lunch. When they return, they can't find their sandcastle anywhere. It has vanished. What has happened?

If you guessed that the tide came in and swallowed Susannah and Peter's castle, congratulations. Tides are the daily rise and fall of the world's oceans. If you've been to the beach you might have noticed that the water creeps up the beach (high tide), then back down (low tide) throughout the day. To find out what causes tides, turn the page.

At high tide more than half of this rocky shore will be under water. Notice the horizontal stripes? To see what they are, turn to page 24.

The constant gravitational pull of the moon and the sun are the main tide makers. The moon's effect is greatest. Even though it is smaller than the sun, it is closer to the Earth and exerts a greater pull. The moon and sun are not strong enough to pull the Earth out of shape, like a piece of toffee. But they do pull at the oceans. As a result, the ocean bulges and creates tides.

To understand tides, you must remember that the Earth does a full rotation once every day, the moon revolves around the Earth once every month, and the moon and Earth rotate around the sun once every year.

Think of the Earth as a ball coated in a layer of water (the oceans).

Now add the moon into the picture. The moon pulls the oceans towards it on the side of the Earth facing it. If you live at Town X, it is high tide. If you live at Town Y, it's low tide. As the Earth revolves, this bulge of water travels around the world following the moon.

MOON

Besides gravitational pull, centrifugal force also contributes to tides. For more about centrifugal force and its effects, try "Magic Water Spinner."

The tides change at Town X throughout each day as the Earth revolves in relation to the moon. Like most places, Town X has two high and two low tides every day. Some places have only one tide a day; others don't have

---

Magic water spinner

When objects (like the Earth or a bucket of water) spin, centrifugal force starts to act. What is centrifugal force? You can see it at work in a spinning cup.

You'll need:
a pencil
a paper cup
scissors
a ruler
string or yarn

1. Use the pencil to punch two holes across from each other near the rim of the paper cup.

2. Cut two pieces of string 60 cm (2 feet) long. Knot them together at one end. Then thread the free ends through the holes in the cup and tie them.
3. Half-fill the cup with water.
4. Hold the knot and swing the cup around in a horizontal circle above your head.

The water stays in the cup as it spins because of centrifugal force. This force causes a spinning object to fly away from the centre that it is turning around. The water in the cup is moving outwards because of centrifugal force, but the cup stops it from flying away. The water of the ocean also bulges outwards because of centrifugal force but is prevented from flying off into space because of the Earth's gravity.

tides at all. Why the variations? When you add shorelines and land masses into the picture, things change a bit. The tilt of the Earth, the Earth's spin and the water depth also influence tides.

As the position of the Earth, sun and moon changes throughout the year, tide heights and times vary. High and low tides don't reach the same level on the beach each day. The tidal range – the difference between high and low tides – is always changing. Every two weeks there are tides with especially big tidal ranges.

These tides are called spring tides and they happen when the Earth, moon and sun are all in line. The combination of both the

sun and the moon's pull on the Earth creates these very high, and very low, tides. Neap tides are just the opposite. They happen when the moon and sun pull from directions that are not in line. On these days, the tidal range is not very large.

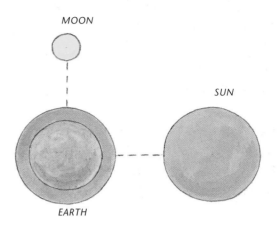

One of the most famous tidal areas in the world is the Bay of Fundy in Nova Scotia and New Brunswick. The difference between high and low tides there can be as much as 15 m (49 feet).

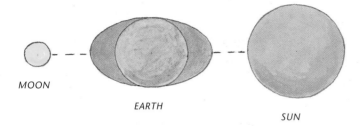

Low tide is a great time to explore tidepools. For more about tidepools, turn to page 30.

Life on a sandy beach

The residents of Oceanview have a problem. Their favourite beach is becoming a popular place for dirt bikers to roar up and down. The bikers argue that nothing lives on this beach, so why worry?
In desperation, the residents hire marine detective Pearl Shelley to find out what, if anything, lives here. Try to help Pearl out. Can you spot six clues that were left for her by the animals that live here?
Turn the page to see how you did.

Where does sand come from?

It gets into everything – your hair, your shoes, your peanut butter sandwich. But what exactly is sand, and where does it come from? Some sand is made as wind and water wear mountains into large boulders, boulders into pebbles and pebbles into grains of sand. Other bits of sand are pieces of shell and hard animal parts worn away by the water.

Take a close look at some sand with a magnifying glass. Can you see different types of tiny rocks? Pass a magnet over the sand. Are any pieces magnetic? They are probably magnetite, a magnetic iron ore. Transparent grains are probably quartz, the most abundant mineral in the Earth's crust. Add a drop of vinegar to your sand. If it fizzes, your sample contains calcium carbonate, the stuff shells are made of. The bubbles you see forming are carbon dioxide.

The beach dwellers revealed

Little did the dirt bikers know that as they roared along, they were riding on the roofs of an underground city. Here are the creatures Pearl Shelley discovered living in the sand.

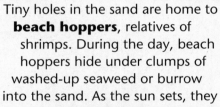

Tiny holes in the sand are home to **beach hoppers**, relatives of shrimps. During the day, beach hoppers hide under clumps of washed-up seaweed or burrow into the sand. As the sun sets, they come out of their burrows and hop along the beach, scavenging on decaying plants and animals.

This coil marks the end of a **lugworm**'s J-shaped burrow. The lugworm swallows sand and mud, digesting the food that is on it and getting rid of the leftovers in this coil. It pumps water through the burrow to bring in fresh sea water.

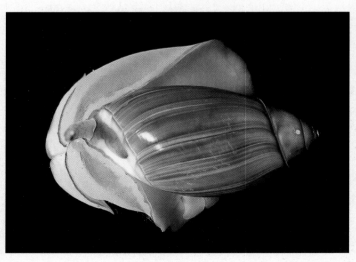

This beautiful **purple olive snail** ploughs through the sand, just under the surface, searching for bits of food. It produces a net of mucus to snag food.

This rubbery ring contains eggs laid by the giant **moon snail**. This snail travels through the sand in search of prey such as clams and olive snails. Then it drills a hole through its victim's shell using its radula, a special "tongue" with spikes. Finally it sucks up the innards of its prey.

A sandy home

As the tide moves in and waves crash on the beach, the grains of sand move and shift. There are no rocks to hold on to, no seaweed for shelter and no tidepools. To survive here most animals must burrow into the sand.

Some creatures are so tiny they can live *between* the grains of sand! Many microscopic animals live in a film of water between sand grains. Some survive by licking the sand to remove tiny particles of food.

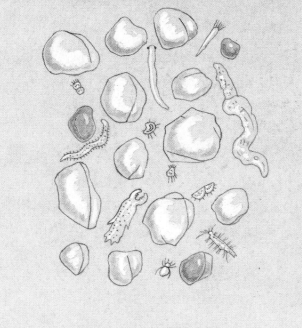

 A squirt of water coming from a hole in the sand means a **clam** is nearby. Clams stick two siphons up to the surface. One sucks up water and food. The squirt you see is waste water being forced out of the second siphon. Clams use their hatchet-shaped foot for burrowing and anchoring in the sand.

Sand dollars are covered in a black "fuzz" of short spines. They use these spines and snakelike, tubular feet to move on the surface of the sand or to burrow deeper down. To avoid being washed away by the tide, young sand dollars eat heavy grains of sand that act like a weight belt to keep them anchored.

Life on the rocks

Pretend for a moment that you are a tiny sea snail living on a rocky shore, where the land and sea meet. This "intertidal zone" is covered with water during high tides and exposed to the air during low tides. It can be a pretty tough place to live.

When the tide is low, you are exposed to the elements (the air, wind, sun, rain and snow). The heat of the sun makes your temperature rise. The winds dry you out. You are also exposed to hungry predators, such as raccoons and gulls.

Life isn't much easier when the tide starts coming in. The first wave of the incoming tide hits you and your temperature plunges. Wave after wave pounds over you, threatening to pull you off the rocks. Predators from the sea begin to hunt. Watch out for that sea star!

Creatures that live in the intertidal zone are well adapted to their changing environment. Some, such as the tiny periwinkle, are almost land creatures. They've developed ways to survive with only the occasional splash of water. Others are very much creatures of the sea. They can tolerate exposure to the air only briefly.

In many places the intertidal zone is divided into distinct bands or sub-zones, each with a different grouping of plants and animals. Which zone a creature lives in depends on how it adapts to three things: exposure, competition for space and food, and predation.

Competition is tough for both space and food, and those less able to compete are driven to live higher up in the intertidal zone.

Predators have a major influence on where creatures live. For example, you won't see many mussels in the area where sea stars live. Mussels are sea stars' favourite food. As you go higher up the intertidal zone, conditions become too harsh for the sea stars. Above this point, mussels can live without danger of being eaten.

Tidepools

Water collects in crevices and hollows, creating pools like the one below. Tidepool dwellers are always covered by sea water, so they don't risk drying out. But rain can make the pool less salty fast, while the sun can overheat the water. Inhabitants must be able to withstand these stresses. For a closer look at a tidepool, see page 30.

The spray zone

This zone gets only splashes of water from breaking waves – unless there is a storm. The few plants and animals that live here are more creatures of the land than of the sea.

The high-tide zone

Here, plants and animals are covered with water during the highest tides but are left high and dry during low tides. The inhabitants of this zone, and the others below it, are experts at hanging on. They have to be – waves crash and break over them with brutal force. Barnacles are common here.

The mid-tide zone

Life is more varied and abundant here than in the higher zones. Plants and animals spend hours at a time either underwater or exposed to the air, as the tide covers and uncovers them once or twice a day.

The low-tide zone

This zone is almost always under water and is only exposed during extremely low tides. It is less changeable than the mid- and high-tide zones, and the animals living here are not as well adapted to exposure. A variety of seaweeds grow in the low-tide zone, providing shelter and food for many animals.

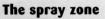

Hanging on

If you visit a rocky sea coast, don't get too close to the water's edge. The crashing surf may be strong enough to knock you off your feet. How do plants and animals in the intertidal zone hang on? Having a streamlined body shape helps – the water simply washes over. But there are other ways of hanging on, too.

◄ **Limpets** and chitons crawl slowly across the rocks in search of algae to eat. To keep from being washed away by pounding waves, they have a powerful foot (see above) that grabs onto the rocks. Some types of limpets return time after time to the same "homeplace" – a spot in the rock where they fit almost perfectly.

Try pulling a **barnacle** off a rock and you're in for a surprise. It's stuck on – tight! Barnacles secrete a cement so powerful that dentists and surgeons are studying it for use in gluing in fillings and mending broken bones. ►

◄ **Mussels** anchor themselves to the rocks with strong threads called byssal threads. (Some people call these threads the "beard" of the mussel.) The threads intrigue scientists because they can harden in water – even salt water. Since human bodies are also salty, the material that byssal threads are made of may be helpful in mending knees and hips. A mussel secretes only enough byssal threads to hang on. In quiet waters, mussels can be picked off with a flick of your finger. On a more exposed shore, you'd need a crowbar.

Goose barnacles have a slender stalk that looks something like a goose's neck. (Long ago, people thought that geese hatched from goose barnacles!) This stalk is tough yet flexible, a bit like a piece of licorice. Instead of resisting the pounding waves, the stalk bends and sways and "goes with the flow." ►

▲ The **sea palm** is so well adapted for strong wave action that it grows only in the roughest water conditions on the most exposed points of land. It has a rugged, strong holdfast to anchor it to the rocks and a strong whiplike stalk that bends with the waves.

◄ This **shore crab** crawls under rocks or into crevices to keep from being washed away. That would be an uncomfortable squeeze for most animals but not for the crab. Its flat body is ideal for fitting into tight places.

Exposed!

If you lived half of your life underwater and half on land, you'd need a lot of gear – everything from a scuba tank and wet suit to dry clothes and a hair dryer. The plants and animals of the intertidal zone don't need special equipment – their bodies are adapted to the hazards of their wet-dry world. What are those hazards?

TOO DRY!

Sun and wind can rob plants and animals of precious body fluids. Especially at risk are sea animals' gills. If a sea creature's gills become dried out, it loses its ability to take oxygen out of the water. Like you, sea creatures must have oxygen.

To stay moist while the tide is out, crabs scuttle into cracks or crevices. Sea stars cluster together in cracks or under overhanging rocks. Other animals hide under a wet bed of seaweed.

Some animals withdraw into their shells. Snails retreat into their shells and close a protective trapdoor, called an operculum, attached to their foot. Chitons and limpets get a firm grip on the rock, which helps seal moisture inside their shells. Mussels and barnacles close their shells up tight.

Sea anemones don't have a shell. To keep moist, they pull in their tentacles and cover themselves with bits of sand and shell to reflect the sun's rays. Prickly **sea urchins** (below) sometimes cover themselves, too.

TOO HOT!

High temperatures can quickly dry out an intertidal creature animal and also affect chemical reactions in its body.

How do intertidal creatures adapt to high temperatures? Limpets may lift their shells slightly off the rocks to allow air to evaporate some of the water stored under their shells. On hot days, barnacles and mussels can often be seen with their shells slightly open – they're cooling off, too. Intertidal animals that can move seek out shelter in cool cracks or damp places.

TOO COLD!

The incoming tide brings instant cool. But winter is another matter.

Gradual cooling gives some animals, such as mussels, time to produce a type of antifreeze. The antifreeze lowers the temperature at which water in their body's tissues freezes, which prevents dangerous ice crystals from forming. But a sudden cold snap may be deadly for many intertidal creatures.

TOO FRESH!

Another big danger is rain. If you put an ocean fish into a pail of fresh water it would die. Fortunately, intertidal creatures have strategies to cope with the low salt content of fresh water. Most use the same tricks they use to avoid exposure – they hide or close up tight. Why are changes in salinity so dangerous to marine creatures? Try "Salt or No Salt?" to find out.

▲ These **goose barnacles** close up tight to avoid drying out.

Salt or no salt?

What happens when sea creatures get rained on? Can they survive in fresh water? Try this experiment to find out the answer.

You'll need:
2 glasses, each containing 250 mL (1 cup) water
10 mL (2 tsp) salt
a spoon
a potato
a table knife
a ruler
a small food scale (optional)
a pencil and paper

1. Stir the salt into one of the glasses of water until it dissolves.

2. Cut two strips of potato the same shape and size. Measure the strips and, if possible, weigh them. Record the measurements.

3. Place one strip in the glass of fresh water and the other in the glass of salt water.

4. Leave strips in overnight. In the morning, measure and weigh them again. What happened?

The potato in fresh water swelled up as it absorbed water. The other strip shrunk as it got rid of water. Why did the potato strips absorb or lose water? To equalize their salt content with the water around them. Potatoes are less salty than the salt water but more salty than fresh water. The potato strip in fresh water swelled because it took in water to become more like the water around it. The potato strip in salt water got smaller because it lost fresh water to become saltier, like the surrounding water.

Water passed into or out of the potato strips to adjust their salt content. The same thing happens to sea creatures. Put a sea creature in fresh water and it will swell with water as it tries to adjust to the water around it. This is why it's better to leave marine creatures where you find them.

Nature's aquariums: Tidepools

Look into a tidepool and you'll find many intertidal creatures. While tidepools may look like an ideal place to escape some of the dangers of life in the intertidal zone, animals and plants living here have their own special problems. The sun can heat up the water in a tidepool; rain can change the salinity (saltiness). Only plants and animals that are well adapted to withstand these changing conditions can survive in tidepools.

Hermit crabs don't have a hard outer shell to protect their abdomens like most crabs, so they have to borrow one. This hermit has taken over an empty snail's shell, which it uses as a mobile home. It will move to a bigger shell as it grows. Often hermit crabs fight over the most desirable homes. Sometimes a crab carries around a "roommate" – an anemone or barnacle that attaches itself to the crab's borrowed shell.

▲ To a **sculpin** there's no place like home. If it is washed out of its tidepool, a homing instinct helps it find its way back. Because of their colouring and small size, sculpins are often hard to spot – unless they are hungry. Then they act like piranhas, gripping onto food and spinning around until a chunk tears off.

▲ **Tube worms**, marine "cousins" of earthworms, build strong tubes of calcium or sand to live in. They stick out their tentacles to feed and breathe. When disturbed, the worms withdraw into their tubes. Some tubeworms have a trapdoor, or operculum, which they shut tight for added protection.

The **sea cucumber** wedges its squishy body into crevices and under rocks – perfect hideaways from predators. The sticky orange tentacles wave in the water and collect food that drifts by. Then the sea cucumber puts a tentacle into its mouth and "licks" it clean. ▶

Be a tidepool explorer

To get a better look at life in a tidepool – or in shallow water – make a waterscope or a dipnet.

Waterscope

You'll need:
a plastic jug or large tin can
a knife or can opener
scissors
plastic wrap
a rubber band or piece of elastic
waterproof tape

1. Ask an adult to cut the bottom out of your container with a knife or can opener. **Important:** make sure you have an adult's help before using a knife.

2. Cut a piece of plastic wrap large enough to cover the bottom of your container.

3. Secure the plastic with a big rubber band or piece of elastic. Make sure the elastic is tight.

4. Tape down the edges of the plastic wrap with the waterproof tape.

5. Try out your waterscope. Put the plastic-wrapped end in the water and look through the open end.

Dipnet

You'll need:
a coat hanger
scissors
an old pair of pantihose
a darning needle threaded with string or wool
a bucket

1. With an adult's help, shape the coat hanger into a circle.

2. Cut one leg off the pantihose. Stretch the open end over the coat hanger.

3. Sew the pantihose leg onto the coat hanger.

4. Fill your bucket with salt water.

5. Try out your dipnet. Gently lift creatures out of their home and have a good look at them in your bucket before returning them.

Seashore safety and etiquette

Follow these guidelines when exploring the home of intertidal creatures – for their safety and yours.

• *Never turn your back on the waves. Large waves can arise suddenly, sweeping people off rocky headlands.*

• *Study the animals where you find them. It is very difficult to keep marine creatures alive away from the beach.*

• *Always return animals and plants to the place you found them.*

• *To minimize the disturbance to burrowing animals, fill in any holes you make in the sand.*

• *Do not forcibly pry off animals and plants that are attached to a rock.*

Intertidal forests

Imagine what the intertidal zone must look like from a snail's perspective. Cracks in the rock would be like the Grand Canyon. A climb uphill might seem like a trek up Mt. Everest. Crawling into a bed of seaweed would be like entering a cool, damp forest of huge trees.

Intertidal seaweed is an important habitat for life on the shore. One of the most common intertidal seaweeds in North America is rockweed, or bladderwrack. Look under a bed of rockweed and you might be surprised by what you find.

Just like intertidal animals, intertidal plants must be able to cope with changes in their home as the tides rise and fall and the seasons change. The heat of a summer's day is no problem for rockweed. It has thick skin to hold in moisture. The higher up the intertidal zone it lives, the thicker its skin. It can survive even if it loses 90 per cent of its water. In cold weather, rockweed can stand having 80 per cent of its body fluids frozen. Once conditions return to normal, so does the plant. Arctic species can spend several months frozen in the sea ice with no apparent damage.

Rockweed photosynthesizes (manufactures food from sunlight) better out of the water than in. This is a valuable survival strategy, since the plant spends most of its life out of the water. When the tide is in, gas-filled "bladders" help keep the plant upright. This means more of the plant is kept out of the shadow of other seaweeds.

Rockweed has even found a way to make sure that intertidal animals don't gobble it up – it produces bad-tasting chemicals called phenols.

Microscopic **tube-dwelling worms** seek out rockweed to settle on when they are young. They often attach themselves to it and spend their entire life there. Look for the tiny white coils of the worm's tube.

The **chiton** (above) and **snails** (below) hold onto the rock under the cool forest of rockweed.

Many smaller **seaweeds** form an understorey, or layer, beneath the canopy of rockweed.

Limpets and **shore crabs** crawl into the rockweed to escape the drying sun and winds.

Tiny **amphipods** cling to the plant. Their camouflage colouring can make them difficult for predators to see.

Radioactive rockweed

In 1986, an accident at the Chernobyl nuclear reactor in the Ukraine released clouds of radioactive material into the atmosphere. Dr. Louis Druehl, a Vancouver botanist, saw a great opportunity for a scientific study. He contacted friends all around the northern hemisphere and asked them to collect rockweed and ship the plants to his lab.

Dr. Druehl wanted to measure the amount of radioactive iodine in the rockweed from the various locations. This way he could measure how fast the radioactivity was moving and what places received most of the radioactive fallout. He found that it took two weeks for the radioactive cloud to reach North America, at Sitka, Alaska. The study also found that plants growing in places with the highest rainfall had the highest amount of radioactive iodine in their tissues.

Studies like this give scientists a good way to learn about air pollution and its effects on plants and animals.

A star's life

Surf's up and so is the tide. Most of the intertidal zone is underwater. Here's what living in the intertidal zone is like for one sea creature, the shore star.

High tide means dinner time for this sea star. What's on the menu today? A snail, chiton, limpet, barnacle or clam? Perhaps a nice tasty mussel? A bed of mussels is nearby. The sea star crawls towards it on hundreds of tube feet. Once there, it drapes itself over a mussel and latches on with an iron grip, prying apart the shell until there is a small opening – all that's needed is a space big enough to slip this page through.

The sea star is ready to eat. But instead of sucking the mussel out of its shell, the sea star squeezes its stomach inside the mussel shell. Then it secretes powerful digestive juices and chows down, only retrieving its stomach when it is done. Just one mussel makes a meal. Now the sea star won't have to eat for several days!

Dinner's over and the tide is starting to retreat. The sea star crawls down to the lower parts of the intertidal zone so it can stay underwater as long as possible. That way it can avoid hungry predators such as gulls. A predator attack needn't mean certain death for the sea

star. As long as part of the central disc – the point where the "arms" meet – is left behind, this "Houdini of the sea" can regenerate (grow) new arms.

For the next six hours, the tide is out and the sea star is exposed to the wind and sun. Fortunately, it has tough, leathery skin to keep moisture in. And sea stars really like togetherness. You'll often see them clustered in large groups under rocks or overhanging ledges. This helps them keep cool and prevents their gills (which are on their back) from drying out.

This sea star is eating a mussel.

A sea star's tube feet

Coral reefs: Sunken homes

Divers have noticed that marine creatures sometimes turn sunken ships into homes. In some places, marine creatures don't wait for a ship to sink. They build their own underwater apartments – coral reefs.

Coral reefs are made up of thousands, sometimes millions, of skeletons of coral polyps. The polyps secrete a hard cup-shaped skeleton to protect their soft bodies. As the coral polyps die, the skeletons remain and more corals build on top of the old skeletons. The largest coral reef in the world is the Great Barrier Reef in Australia. It's so big that astronauts can see it from the moon!

Most coral need help to build these spectacular reefs, and they get it from a microscopic, single-celled algae called zooxanthellae. The zooxanthellae grow in the coral – they are what give the coral its colour. In exchange for nutrients and a place to live, the zooxanthellae help the coral secrete calcium carbonate for its skeleton.

Since zooxanthellae need light, reef-building corals grow best in water that is shallow, warm and clear. That's why most coral reefs are found in tropical waters. There are also many types of corals that don't build reefs growing in tropical and cooler oceans.

Coral reefs are full of nooks and crannies – ideal housing for marine creatures.

Most corals grow in large colonies. They are named according to their shapes. Can you find a **plate**, **brain**, **star** and **elkhorn coral** in this picture? Answers on page 78.

Coralline algae, a special type of hardened seaweed, help cement the corals in the reef together.

Look for **shrimp fish** hiding head down among the spines of the **sea urchin**. Their narrow bodies are perfectly camouflaged. ▶

▲ **Giant clams** can grow up to 1.2 m (4 feet) wide and weigh up to 263 kg (580 pounds). Like the coral, they also have zooxanthellae living in them.

Many **coral reef fish** are brightly coloured. Spots and stripes disrupt their profile, making them harder for predators to spot.

The **seahorse** uses its tail to grasp on to corals or plants while it searches for food. Roving eyes allow the seahorse to look for a meal with one eye while watching for predators with the other.

◄ Some fish and shrimp act as cleaners on the coral reef. The striped **cleaner wrasse** on the left has a cleaning station. When a "customer" comes along, the cleaner wrasse picks away its parasites and any infected tissue around wounds. Often the host fish will even allow the cleaner to enter its mouth and gills.

◄ The tentacles of **sea anemones** can give a deadly sting. So what is this **clown fish** doing here? After a series of minor stings, it becomes immune to the stings. It hides among the anemone's tentacles for protection. In return, the clown fish acts as bait, luring other fish within reach of the anemone.

Seaweeds: Underwater forests

Tall plants sway above you, even though there is no breeze. It is completely silent – no birds chirp and no leaves rustle. Suddenly, a fish swims by. You are in an underwater forest of red, green and brown seaweeds. It's time to explore.

Some seaweeds cling to rocks like tiny tufts of moss. Others, such as the giant kelp you see here, can grow as tall as a ten-storey building.

Seaweeds provide food and shelter for many ocean creatures. The kelp forest serves as a nursery for many species of animals, particularly fish. Many invertebrates such as snails settle as larvae on the kelp blades and wait to develop into adults. What other animals can you find living in this kelp forest?

The **blades** reach up and out to capture as much sunlight as possible. They use the sun to manufacture food just as land plants do. This is called photosynthesis. The blades often form a canopy in the upper level of the forest and are a place where fish, birds and marine mammals such as seals, sea otters and grey whales can find shelter and food.

Seaweeds have **holdfasts** instead of roots to anchor them to the ocean floor so they won't get washed away by the waves. Land plants need roots to take up water and nutrients from the soil. Since seaweeds are bathed in water all the time, the entire plant can absorb nutrients and water. Crabs, brittle stars, worms and clams find shelter in the holdfasts.

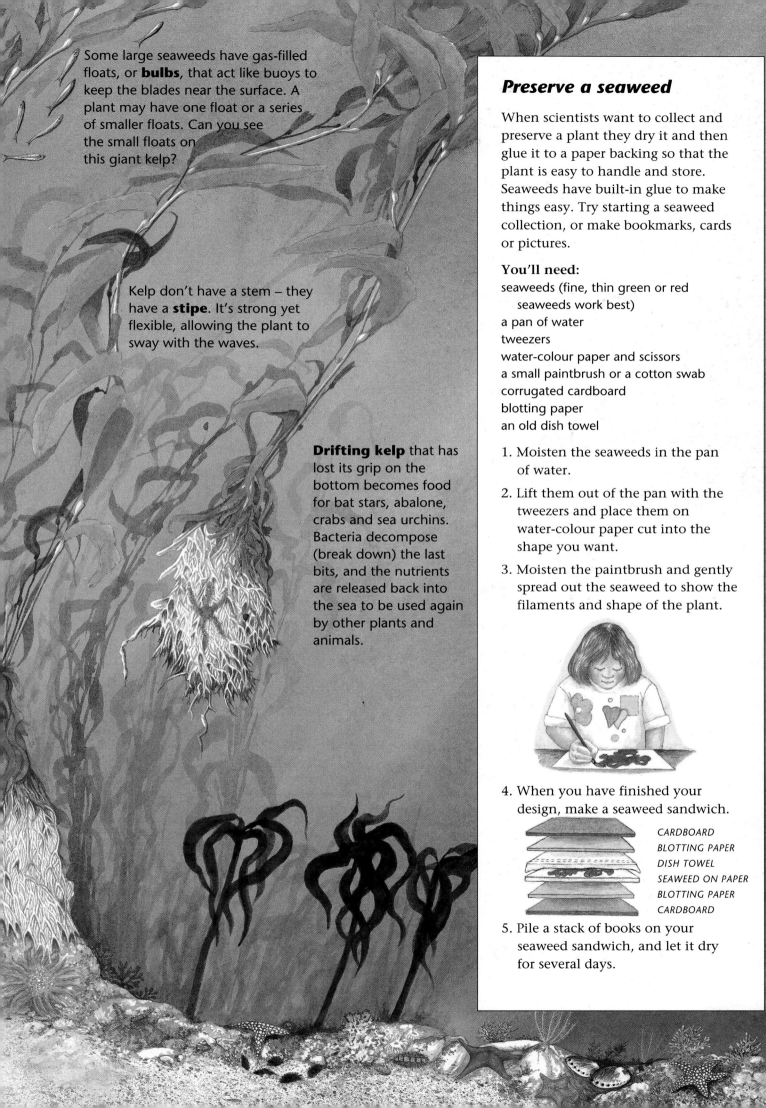

Some large seaweeds have gas-filled floats, or **bulbs**, that act like buoys to keep the blades near the surface. A plant may have one float or a series of smaller floats. Can you see the small floats on this giant kelp?

Kelp don't have a stem – they have a **stipe**. It's strong yet flexible, allowing the plant to sway with the waves.

Drifting kelp that has lost its grip on the bottom becomes food for bat stars, abalone, crabs and sea urchins. Bacteria decompose (break down) the last bits, and the nutrients are released back into the sea to be used again by other plants and animals.

Preserve a seaweed

When scientists want to collect and preserve a plant they dry it and then glue it to a paper backing so that the plant is easy to handle and store. Seaweeds have built-in glue to make things easy. Try starting a seaweed collection, or make bookmarks, cards or pictures.

You'll need:
seaweeds (fine, thin green or red
   seaweeds work best)
a pan of water
tweezers
water-colour paper and scissors
a small paintbrush or a cotton swab
corrugated cardboard
blotting paper
an old dish towel

1. Moisten the seaweeds in the pan of water.

2. Lift them out of the pan with the tweezers and place them on water-colour paper cut into the shape you want.

3. Moisten the paintbrush and gently spread out the seaweed to show the filaments and shape of the plant.

4. When you have finished your design, make a seaweed sandwich.

CARDBOARD
BLOTTING PAPER
DISH TOWEL
SEAWEED ON PAPER
BLOTTING PAPER
CARDBOARD

5. Pile a stack of books on your seaweed sandwich, and let it dry for several days.

Going down

Dr. André Martel is getting ready to take a dive. He is a marine biologist (a scientist who studies ocean life) and his laboratory is the ocean. Join Dr. Martel, and budding biologist Liz, to learn about the strange world below the waves.

Liz: How deep can you dive in that gear?
Dr. Martel: 30 to 40 m (98 to 130 feet) is the maximum depth for safe scuba-diving. You're limited by the amount of air you can carry and other potential dangers, such as getting nitrogen gas in your bloodstream. There isn't really much to see beyond those depths anyway. For my marine research I usually stay in the top 10 to 20 m (33 to 66 feet). Sunlight penetrates well there, so there are lots of seaweeds growing. All types of animals find food and shelter in the seaweeds.

Liz: What does it feel like when you go underwater?
Dr. Martel: At first you feel the pressure from the water all around you. Your diving suit sticks to your skin and your eardrums start to hurt. It's very quiet and calm underwater, but the sound of your own breathing is quite loud. You're also very light and buoyant when you dive. You tend to sink quite slowly. It can get pretty cold, too, even if you are wearing proper gear.

Liz: What can you see when you're down there?
Dr. Martel: I like to dive along kelp beds where there are crab, seaweeds and schools of fish. The seaweeds sway back and forth with the surge from the waves. That's very striking. The most common animals I see are sea stars, sea urchins, hermit crabs and snails. Some days it seems like you can see forever underwater, but then, often just a few days later, it's so murky you can hardly see your hand in front of your face.

Liz: What causes that murkiness?
Dr. Martel: It's mostly caused by plankton. Plankton is made up of microscopic plants, called phytoplankton, and microscopic animals, called zooplankton. Plankton live in the water and float with the currents. Sometimes large patches of phytoplankton move into an area, making the water look murky green. When the days start to get long in the spring, the phytoplankton grow quickly, or "bloom." There may be millions of phytoplankton in a cubic metre (yard) of sea water. That doesn't make for very good diving.

Liz: What are you doing when you're down there?
Dr. Martel: I study the behaviour of marine snails. When I'm diving, I collect the snails and the seaweeds they live on in sample bags and take them back to the lab to have a closer look. I'm particularly interested in the type of habitat the young snails choose and how they move from one place to another.

Scuba gear

Dr. Martel can do a lot of his research underwater because he can scuba dive. Scuba, which stands for Self-Contained Underwater Breathing Apparatus, allows divers to stay under by breathing from a tank of compressed air.

A **snorkel** is for breathing at the surface.

The **mask** keeps a layer of air between a diver's eyes and the water, so that he can focus better.

The diver pumps air in and out of a special vest called a **buoyancy compensator** to help him hover at any depth or float at the surface.

To keep from bobbing up to the surface, the diver wears a **weight belt** weighing between 7 and 13.5 kg (15 and 30 pounds).

The **regulator** controls how much air the diver breathes as he changes depth.

This **spare regulator** is for a diving buddy in distress.

Gauges tell the diver how deep he is and how much air is left in his tank.

This **dry suit** keeps the water out.

A **light** and **knife** are for safety.

Fins help propel the diver faster in the water.

SEA SOUP

When Dr. Martel gets back to his lab and puts his samples under the microscope, this is what he sees. These are the

larvae (young) of the snails he studies. These larvae spend part of their life as plankton. Plankton is a Greek word that means "wandering." It's a good name for these plants and animals, which drift on the ocean currents. One litre (1 quart) of sea water may contain as many as 10 million or more plankton.

Plankton is a bit like veggie-beef soup – plants (the phytoplankton) and animals (the zooplankton), some large and some small, all float around in a liquid.

Phytoplankton have an important job. Like all green plants, they create oxygen as they make food from the energy of the sun. Oxygen, of course, is necessary for life on Earth and in the oceans. So take a deep breath and thank the phytoplankton.

Plankton is also an important food for many sea

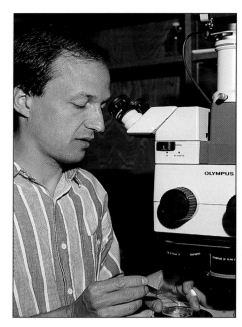

creatures. Small animals eat the plankton and they in turn are eaten by larger animals. This is called a food chain. (For more about food chains, see page 70.) Without plankton, there would be few living creatures in the oceans.

Who's who

What do you think this will be when it grows up? It is the larval stage of a red rock crab. While it is a larva, it will drift like other plankton, "hitchhiking" on the ocean currents.

Many other sea creatures are only plankton for one stage of their lives, their larval stage. Can you match up the planktonic larvae (numbered on the left) with the adults they become (on the right)? Answers on page 78.

Meet some plankton

Some plankton are so small you'd need a high-powered microscope to see them. These plankton are big enough to see with the naked eye. Look for them floating on or near the ocean surface, moving with the wind and currents.

This **purple sea snail** blows bubbles at a rate of one per minute and joins them together to make a raft. Then it hangs upside down from the raft, which floats at the surface.

This **Portuguese-man-of-war jellyfish** is actually a group of small polyps living together in a colony. Some polyps make the float that blows in the wind carrying the others along. Others make up the tentacles and capture food with special stinging cells. The long tentacles can trail for as much as 30 m (98 feet) and can give a deadly sting.

This **sunfish** can grow up to 3.3 m (11 feet) long and weigh more than 1410 kg (3102 pounds). It is the largest bony fish alive – and one of the slowest. Rather than swimming, it becomes part of the plankton and drifts with the currents. Its favourite food is another drifter – the jellyfish.

Something fishy

Suppose you met a Martian who wanted to know what a fish was. How would you describe fish to distinguish them from other animals? If you said that fish live in water (are aquatic), are cold-blooded (unlike whales, dolphins and other mammals, which are warm-blooded), breathe using gills (not lungs) and use fins instead of arms or legs to move, you'd be right!

There are more types of fish in the world than all the mammals and birds combined. Most fish have a rigid skeleton made of bone – you can see the skeleton after a fish dinner. They are called bony fish.

There are thousands of different kinds of bony fish. Some feed on plankton that they filter out of the water, while others are ferocious hunters. Some are round like balloons, and others look more like snakes. One fish even looks like a miniature horse. Yes – the sea horse is a fish!

Despite their differences, most fish share some basic equipment. This rock fish has "the works."

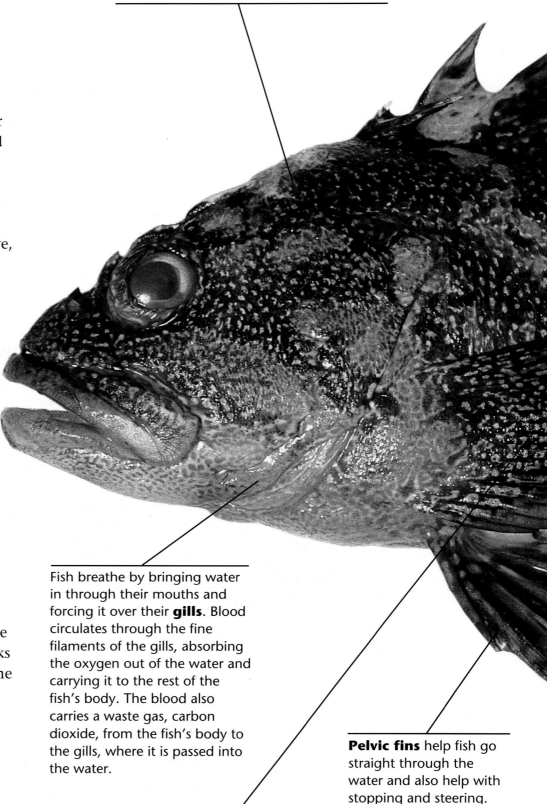

Special cells called **chromatophores** give the fish its colour. Many fish can change the size, shape and colour of these cells to help them blend in with their surroundings.

Fish breathe by bringing water in through their mouths and forcing it over their **gills**. Blood circulates through the fine filaments of the gills, absorbing the oxygen out of the water and carrying it to the rest of the fish's body. The blood also carries a waste gas, carbon dioxide, from the fish's body to the gills, where it is passed into the water.

Pelvic fins help fish go straight through the water and also help with stopping and steering.

Most fish use a pair of **pectoral fins** for steering and stopping. By extending one pectoral fin forward, a fish can change direction. By extending both fins forward, it puts on the brakes.

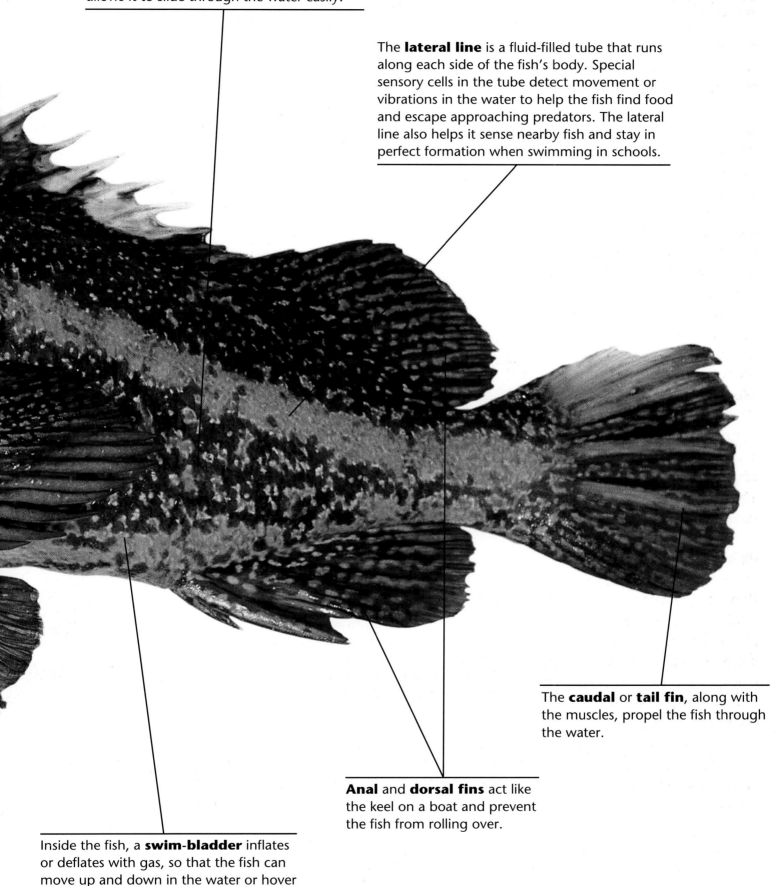

Scales act like a protective coat of armour. A thin, slimy covering of mucus over the scales helps protect the fish from disease and allows it to slide through the water easily.

The **lateral line** is a fluid-filled tube that runs along each side of the fish's body. Special sensory cells in the tube detect movement or vibrations in the water to help the fish find food and escape approaching predators. The lateral line also helps it sense nearby fish and stay in perfect formation when swimming in schools.

The **caudal** or **tail fin**, along with the muscles, propel the fish through the water.

Anal and **dorsal fins** act like the keel on a boat and prevent the fish from rolling over.

Inside the fish, a **swim-bladder** inflates or deflates with gas, so that the fish can move up and down in the water or hover in one place.

Be a fish detective

Next time you see a fish or have one for dinner, use your powers of deduction to learn more about it. Here are some clues to look for.

TAIL SHAPE: A SPEED CLUE

Tail fins can tell you how fast a fish swims. Fish with narrow, crescent-shaped tail fins are very fast swimmers. Species with square or rounded tails can manoeuvre well and have short, quick bursts of speed.

THE MOUTH: A FOOD CLUE

The position of a fish's mouth can tell you a lot about how and where it feeds. If the mouth is pointed upwards, the fish is probably a surface feeder. A mouth on the underside of the fish probably means it scours the bottom for food. This **ratfish**, for example, cruises the bottom looking for snails and clams to munch on.

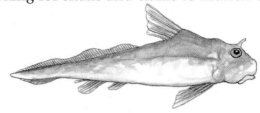

The shape and size of the teeth and mouth can also give valuable clues to the type of food fish prefer. Some fish have teeth that crush or grind. Others have mouths that act like sieves or skewers. This **trumpetfish** uses its long nose and tiny teeth like tweezers to pick small animals out of hiding places.

BODY SHAPE: A HABITAT CLUE

The shape of a fish can also give you a clue to where it lives. Try to match the creatures below with their habitats. Answers on page 78.

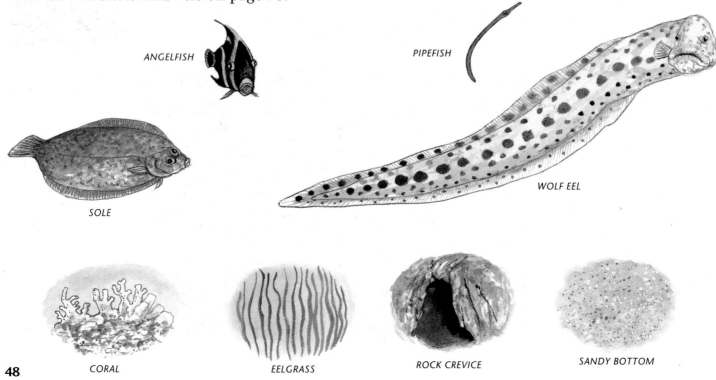

ANGELFISH

PIPEFISH

SOLE

WOLF EEL

CORAL

EELGRASS

ROCK CREVICE

SANDY BOTTOM

48

COLOURATION: A SURVIVAL CLUE

Many fish have special colours and patterns that help them hide from predators.

Fish with countershading have a dark upper surface and a lighter lower surface. Viewed from above, the fish "disappears" into the darkness below. Seen from below, it blends into the lighter colours of the water and sky.

SCALES: AN AGE CLUE

A close look at the scales of a fish under a magnifying glass can tell you its age. Each major ring usually indicates one year's growth. Fish scales also tell scientists a lot about disease, pollution and the amount of food the fish ate.

▲ Fish with disruptive colouration have patterns that break up, or disrupt, their body shapes. This makes them more difficult to see.

▲ False eye spots on the tail or hind end make it difficult to tell whether the fish is coming or going.

◄ Some fish can change the size and shape of their colour cells to blend in with their environment. This blending in is called camouflage.

Fishy art

Long ago, Japanese fishermen used the technique of *gyotaku* to record their catch. They would brush paint on their fish, then press the fish on a piece of paper. This fish print provided a "picture" of a fisherman's catch before the camera became widely available. You can do *gyotaku*, too. Rinse off your fish immediately after printing and you can cook it for dinner.

You'll need:
a fresh, raw, whole fish (rough, scaly fish work best)
paper towels
newspaper
straight pins or modelling clay
2 paintbrushes – 1 medium, 1 small
water-based paints (If you want to eat the fish later, you must use water-based, non-toxic paints.)
white newsprint, water-colour paper or rice-paper

1. Rinse the fish under the tap.
   Carefully dry it with a paper towel – don't rub the scales off.

2. Place the fish on newspaper and spread the fins out. If you need to, use the pins or modelling clay to hold the fins out.

3. Brush on a thin coating of paint. Start at the head and work down to the tail. Don't paint over the eye. Brush again from tail to head to get the paint under the scales.

4. Place the paper carefully on top of the fish. Press firmly over the entire surface. Rub gently, then carefully remove the paper.

5. Use the small brush to paint in the eyeball on your print. A black circle surrounded by a rim of yellow makes the eye stand out well.

6. Most fish can be printed several times. Remember to wash off the paint immediately after printing if you are planning to cook and eat the fish.

ST. PAUL'S SCHOOL
PETERBOROUGH

Fish in the living room

Try your hand at camouflage by hiding camouflaged fish in your house.

You'll need:
white paper
crayons or coloured pencils
scissors

1. Cut out a shape of a fish (it doesn't have to be perfect).

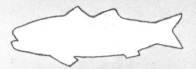

2. Choose a background in your house such as a couch, carpet or bedspread. Start with something that has a plain-coloured background. See if you can colour your fish so it will be camouflaged in its surroundings. Challenge a friend to find the hidden fish.

3. This time choose a colourful patterned background, maybe a bedspread or tablecloth. Cut out and colour another fish, trying to match the pattern and colour. Can your friend find this fish?

JAWS! (and eyes and skin and tails and...)

Think of sharks and what comes to mind? Ripping, tearing jaws? If so, you're in for a surprise. Most of the more than 360 species of sharks are harmless to people. Ready for another surprise? Sharks are boneless! Sharks do have a skeleton, but it is very different from that of other fish. A shark's skeleton is made of cartilage, the same stuff you have in your ears and nose, while other fish have skeletons that are made of bone.

Sharks are full of surprises that make them superbly adapted to life in the oceans.

Sharks can almost see in the dark thanks to a layer of reflective cells behind their eyes called the **tapetum**. The tapetum acts like a mirror and reflects all available light back into the eye – so the light stimulates the shark's eye twice. You can see the tapetum if you have a cat. Watch the tapetum reflecting when a bright light shines into the cat's eyes at night.

Up to two-thirds of a shark's brain weight is devoted to detecting smell. No wonder. Sharks rely on their keen sense of smell to find food, and some can smell even a tiny bit of food as far as 1.6 km (1 mile) away. Also on their snouts are special sensory organs called the **ampullae of Lorenzini** that can pick up the electrical impulses animals give off as their muscles work.

Sharks use and lose thousands of **teeth** during a lifetime. Most sharks don't have to wait long for a replacement, though. They can have up to 20 rows of teeth waiting to grow in and take the place of lost teeth.

Shark **skin** is covered with tiny rough scales that look like teeth. In some species, the skin is rough enough to give you a good cut. This rough skin reduces water turbulence around sharks' bodies and lets them slip through the water more easily.

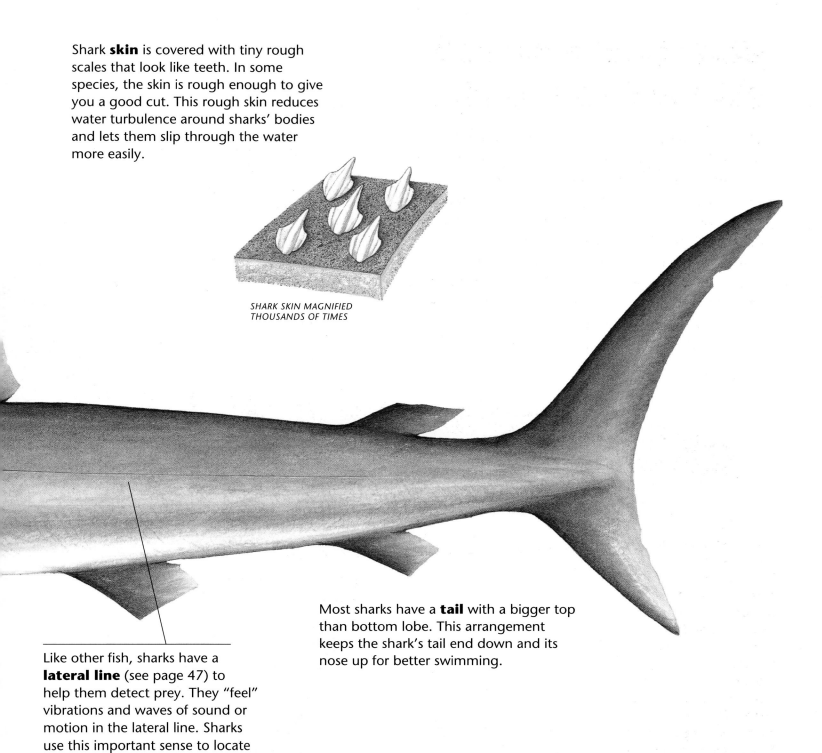

SHARK SKIN MAGNIFIED
THOUSANDS OF TIMES

Most sharks have a **tail** with a bigger top than bottom lobe. This arrangement keeps the shark's tail end down and its nose up for better swimming.

Like other fish, sharks have a **lateral line** (see page 47) to help them detect prey. They "feel" vibrations and waves of sound or motion in the lateral line. Sharks use this important sense to locate injured and struggling prey.

Shark stories

Underwater filmmakers Ron and Valerie Taylor and friend John Harding were heading home on stormy seas after a day of filming. John was standing on the bow of the boat, when he spotted a large dark shape in the water ahead. As the boat crested the next wave, a huge black dorsal fin broke the surface. There was no doubt. It was a shark.

Because of the huge size of the dorsal fin, the filmmakers thought it must be a white pointer shark, one of the most dreaded sharks in the world and a species that had attacked four of their friends. The three filmmakers decided to frighten the shark away to make the waters safe for themselves and other divers.

They pulled the boat ahead of the shark and jumped in with their guns. At first, they could see nothing. They looked around nervously. Suddenly, out of the darkness, loomed a head as wide as a small car. Their dread turned to delight – it was a rare whale shark, the largest shark in the world.

Even though it was huge – about 15 m (50 feet) long – the shark didn't frighten the divers. Whale sharks are plankton feeders and don't have the huge sharp teeth and bad reputation that made people fear other sharks.

Valerie decided to hitch a ride on the shark and grabbed its metre- (yard-) high dorsal fin. The shark didn't seem to mind. Over the course of the afternoon all three divers hitched rides on the shark, which they nicknamed Wimpy. It was a day the divers would never forget. When they reluctantly parted company with Wimpy, the shark had taken them 8 km (5 miles) from where they had first entered the water.

The Taylors are still filming underwater. Their favourite subjects? You guessed it, sharks! Today, the Taylors work hard to educate people about sharks and the fact that very few species are actually dangerous. Valerie swims regularly with sharks, sometimes in specially designed armour but often without any protection at all.

The **cookie-cutter shark** attacks by grabbing onto its prey with its sharp teeth and twisting. This leaves a hole the shape of a cookie.

The tiny **dwarf shark** is small enough to fit in a shoe box.

The **thresher shark** uses its long whiplike tail to herd schools of fish into a tight group so it can get more of a meal in one gulp. It can also use its tail to kill or stun prey.

The **sawshark** uses its long snout to pry up and stun fish, snails or crabs.

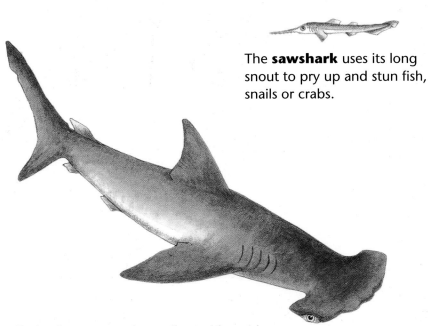

By having eyes and nostrils at either side of its head, the **hammerhead shark** gets a broader range of sight and smell.

The shark arm murder

Imagine the surprise of aquarium owners in Australia when a tiger shark they had caught vomited up the arm of a man! On the arm was a tattoo of two boxers. The tattoo told police that the arm belonged to James Smith, a man who had mysteriously disappeared. On closer examination, however, police discovered that it wasn't a shark that had taken off James Smith's arm, but a knife! Mr. Smith had been murdered. Mr. Smith's murderer has never been found.

Some sharks will eat just about anything. A bottle of wine, a porcupine, a raincoat, part of a horse, rope, a suit of armour, a chest of jewellery, boat cushions, a crocodile's head, a wallet, a hubcap, a yellow-bellied cuckoo and a chicken coop have all been found in sharks' stomachs.

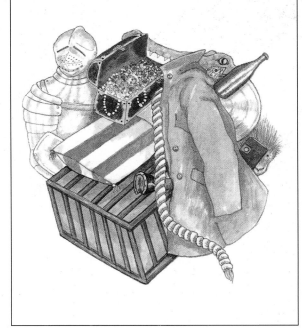

Shark cousins: Skates and rays

You are waist-deep in water, about to take a step, when a shadowy creature erupts out of the sandy bottom and flies towards deeper water. Lucky you! You've just had a close encounter with a skate.

Like their shark cousins, skates and rays are boneless fish. They have a skeleton made of cartilage instead of calcium. Because their bodies are flat, they can lie motionless on the bottom and almost disappear. On the move, their large winglike fins make them look as though they are flying through the water. Most have long thin tails that they use for balance and steering – and sometimes for protection. Ready to meet some members of this unusual fish family?

A devil of a fish ►
A "wingspan" of 8 m (26 feet) makes the **manta ray** the largest species of ray. It is a filter feeder, straining plankton and small fish out of the water. Its large fins, called feeding fins, direct food and water into its mouth. Because the fins look like horns, some people call the ray "devilfish."

Hide and seek ▼
The **long-nose skate** buries itself in the sand, waiting for its next meal of crab, worms or shellfish. Its flat body shape and sandy colour are great camouflage. If a skate tried to breathe through its mouth, it would choke on sand. Instead, it has two special holes called spiracles behind its eyes which take in water to pass over its gills.

Vacuum feeder ▼
The **bat ray** sucks up its prey from the ocean floor. To find food, it flaps its wings, stirring up the sand and uncovering hiding animals. When it finds a spot with lots of food, it settles in and slurps.

Jawless fish

There is one more group of fish besides the true bony fish and the cartilagenous fish (sharks and their cousins the skates and rays) – fish without jaws. Instead of chewing jaws, **lampreys** and **hagfish** have round sucking mouths, often equipped with dozens of tiny barbs. Lampreys latch onto fish or whales and suck their blood.

Hagfish have even more unusual dining habits. They feed on dead and dying fish. They squirm into their prey through the mouth or anus and eat from the inside out until there is just a "bag-o'-bones" left. When distressed, hagfish release huge amounts of slime – they can easily fill a bucket in minutes! This behaviour earned them another name, the slime eel.

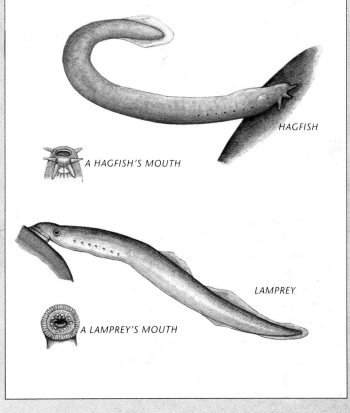

HAGFISH

A HAGFISH'S MOUTH

LAMPREY

A LAMPREY'S MOUTH

The tale of a tail ▼
The **stingray** has a long whiplike tail equipped with a stiff spike. If the stingray is disturbed, the tail whips up and the daggerlike spike is used to sting the disturber. The sting can kill small creatures but, fortunately, is rarely fatal to humans.

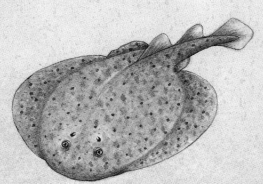

◄ Fish power!
Electric rays such as this **torpedo ray** have electric organs on the sides of their heads that can produce enough electricity to knock you off your feet! The ray positions its prey between its "wings" and stuns it. Scientists think that their electric ability may also help torpedo rays navigate.

57

Marine mammals

Although they live in the ocean, whales, seals, dolphins, porpoises and other marine mammals are more like us than like fish. They are warm-blooded, breathe air and give birth to live young, which they care for and nurse.

Seals, **sea lions** and **walruses** are pinnipeds (meaning "feather-footed"). They rest, mate and give birth on land, and spend the rest of their time in the ocean.

SEA LION

WALRUS

Sea otters are actually members of the weasel family. They spend almost all their time in the ocean.

SEA OTTER

SEAL

Manatees and **dugongs** spend their entire life in the water, in shallow and subtropical coastal areas. These large, docile animals eat only plants.

PORPOISE

DOLPHIN

WHALE

DUGONG

MANATEE

Whales, **dolphins** and **porpoises** never come ashore. Their life is truly a marine experience. Scientists call these animals cetaceans.

From land to sea

Marine mammals have a lot in common with land mammals. In fact, their ancestors lived on land millions of years ago. They took to living in the sea when food and habitat became available for them there. What changes did land mammals undergo to become sea mammals?

STREAMLINING

Over millions of years, marine mammals became streamlined, so they could move through the water more easily. Necks, arms and legs – any parts hanging off the body – were tucked up close.

FLIPPERS AND FINS

Seals and sea lions live both in the water and on land. They need limbs that enable them to swim *and* walk.

Sea lions (see photo this page) and fur seals can walk on land by rotating their rear flippers under their bodies and walking along on all fours. Other seals can't support themselves on their flippers. Instead, they wiggle along on their bellies.

In the water these animals move quite differently, too. Seals swim with side-to-side movements of their rear flippers. Sea lions flap their front flippers and move in a flying motion.

Whales, dolphins and porpoises spend all their lives in the water. They don't need legs to help them walk on land. Their forelimbs are smaller and flatter, and their hind limbs have been replaced with large, horizontal tail flukes for lots of swimming power.

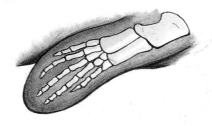

The bones of a marine mammal's flipper look like the bones of our hands and arms. This is an important clue linking marine mammals to life on land.

BREATHING

One of the biggest challenges facing the mammals that took to the sea was breathing. Fish have gills to take oxygen from the water, but mammals don't. They have lungs and must come up to the surface to take a breath of air. If they can't, they will drown. In order to stay underwater for long periods of time, marine mammals have developed extra oxygen-carriers in their blood and a greater blood volume. As they start to run out of oxygen, their bodies automatically send oxygen where it's most needed – to the heart, brain and lungs. Their heart rate slows right down to reduce blood flow to areas where it is not vital. When diving, a seal's heart rate might drop from a resting rate of 100 beats a minute to a diving rate of 10 beats a minute.

KEEPING WARM

As land mammals became marine mammals, they needed new ways to keep warm – water carries away body heat faster than air does.

Walruses have a layer of blubber (fat) up to 15 cm (6 inches) thick to keep them warm and buoyant in frigid Arctic waters. To see how blubber works, try "Fat Insulation" on page 61. Blubber also serves as fuel, which is useful since many species don't eat for part of the year.

Seals and sea lions have both fur and blubber. The fur keeps them warm out of the water and helps protect them from the rough rocks.

Instead of blubber, sea otters have super-thick fur – up to a million hairs in an area the size of a quarter. Otters groom constantly to fluff up the fur closest to their skin. Air trapped in this under-fur helps keep water away from the otter's skin.

To keep from inhaling water, many marine mammals have nostrils that close up tight when they dive.

Whales, dolphins and porpoises have a single or double blowhole on top of their heads instead of nostrils on the front. Why? So they don't have to lift their huge heads out of the water to breathe.

◄ Because of their luxurious fur, **sea otters** were almost hunted to extinction along the Pacific coast of North America during the eighteenth and nineteenth centuries. They are now protected and their numbers are growing slowly. But otters still have one deadly enemy – oil. A small patch of oil on its fur can kill an otter because it puts a "hole" in its layer of insulation.

Fat insulation

To see how blubber can keep sea mammals warm, raid the kitchen for a blubber substitute – lard.

You'll need:
a large bowl of water and ice cubes
lard

1. Stick your finger in the ice-cold water. How long can you keep it there before the cold becomes unbearable?
2. Dry your finger and let it warm up. Now cover your finger evenly with a thick layer of lard.
3. Put your finger in the ice water again. Does it get cold as quickly? The lard acts like blubber and keeps you from losing precious body heat.

Marine mammal marvels

HOLD THAT POSE

Whale researchers keep track of whales by taking photographs of them. They know that each whale has distinctive features. Each **killer whale**, for example, has a unique dorsal fin and saddle patch (the white patch behind the dorsal fin). Humpback whales have unique white patches and scratches on the underside of their tail flukes. Using these body markings, research-ers can identify individual whales and learn how far an animal travels, how long it lives and other important information.

DIVING MACHINES

All marine mammals dive for brief periods of time to find their food, but a few take diving to extremes. **Sperm whales** have dived as deep as 3000 m (9843 feet) in search of their favourite food, the deep-water squid. A dive this deep might take 90 minutes.

MARINE MAMMAL MUSIC

Many marine mammals make sounds underwater to communicate. The **beluga whale** vocalizes so much that it's sometimes called the sea canary. Researchers use a hydrophone (an underwater microphone) to pick up underwater sounds, which they record and analyse.

BIG EATER

There are 39 species of whales, ranging from the 2.5-m (8-foot) long pygmy sperm whale to the **blue whale**, the largest animal alive. Eating only shrimplike creatures called krill, blue whales can grow up to 28 m (92 feet) long and weigh as much as 24 elephants.

UNICORNS?

Males (and sometimes females) of the **Arctic narwhal** grow a spiralled tusk up to 2 m (6 feet) long. The tusk grows from the skull through the upper lip of the animal.

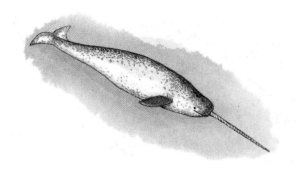

MISTAKEN FOR A MERMAID

Manatees and dugongs are the only marine mammals that eat mostly plants. A manatee can eat up to 45 kg (100 pounds) of vegetation a day. Because they tend to feed upright in the water with their arms out, manatees and dugongs have sometimes been mistaken for mermaids!

MANATEE

FINDING FOOD

Many whales are toothless and instead use **baleen** to strain food from the water. Feel the roof of your mouth with your tongue. Those ridges you feel are where baleen grows from in whales. After the whale takes a mouthful of food and water, it uses its huge tongue to force the water out through the baleen – just like squirting water through your teeth. The food gets caught on the inner fringe of the baleen and is swallowed.

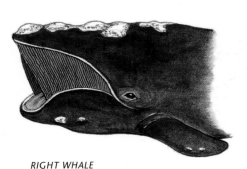

BALEEN

RIGHT WHALE

Whale and fish

Toothed cetaceans, such as dolphins and killer whales, use sound to "see." This is called echolocation. They produce rapid pulses and clicks that bounce off objects in their path. The returning echoes let animals know the size, shape, travel speed and direction of the object in front of them. How good would you be at sounding out prey? Try this game and see.

You'll need:
two or more players (the more the better)
a blindfold

1. Choose one person to be the whale and another to be the fish. Other players can form a circle around the playing area.

2. The whale puts on a blindfold.

3. The fish can move, but he or she must always stay within 3 m (10 feet) of the whale. When the whale shouts out "Whale!" the fish must call out "Fish!" Using these calls, the whale tries to catch the fish.

You are using your ears to find the fish. Whales don't have ears with big lobes to receive sound. Instead, sound enters their jawbone and travels along an oil-filled channel to the inner ear, where it is relayed to the brain.

The deep sea

Scientists divide the open ocean into different zones according to the amount of light. The depths of the zones vary widely from place to place, depending on the clarity of the water. But one thing is certain – the deeper you go, the colder and darker it gets. The pressure is intense too. Still, many creatures can survive deep down in the ocean.

The **sunlit zone** is the depth to which sunlight penetrates. Most ocean life, including all marine plants, is found in this zone.

No light penetrates the **deep-sea zone**. It is totally dark, extremely cold and the intense water pressure could crush many creatures. Even though life is harsh, scientists are discovering more and more life here. What kind of life? See "Hot Vents," then turn to page 68 to discover more deep-sea wonders.

The deepest part of the ocean, found in the Mindanao Trench, is 11 524 m (37 808 feet) deep – much deeper than Mt. Everest is high!

The longest chain of mountains on Earth is underwater. The Mid-Atlantic Ridge stretches more than 64 372 km (40 000 miles). You can see part of this chain where the mountains break through the surface to make the islands of Iceland and the Azores.

In the **midwater** or **twilight zone**, light is very faint, undetectable to our eyes. Many of the animals in this zone swim upwards in the evening to feed in the waters of the lower sunlit zone and move into deeper waters during the day.

Hot vents

Imagine Dr. Verena Tunnicliffe's excitement when she rode down to the ocean floor in a submersible and discovered a whole new community of animals. In 1988 Dr. Tunnicliffe, a Canadian biologist, and her associates were on an expedition to study hydrothermal (hot water) vents on the ocean floor off the west coast of Canada.

Hot vents form where the sea floor splits apart or pushes together. Cold water seeps into the cracks in the Earth's crust and is heated by boiling hot magma under the crust. The hot water is forced up through the sea floor at temperatures as high as 400°C (752°F). Often the super-heated water shoots out of huge underwater chimneys, or "smokers."

Up here on the surface, the sun provides the energy for plants to grow. The plants supply us with food. But in the ocean depths there is no sunlight. Instead, bacteria around the hot vents use chemicals from the hot water to make food. Many hot-vent creatures such as shrimps, sea spiders and clams feast on these bacteria. Giant tube worms (below) couldn't "eat" even if they wanted to – they don't have mouths. Instead, the worms keep a supply of bacteria inside their body to create their food.

Exploring the ocean depths

Over the years, undersea explorers have come up with weird, wacky and sometimes wonderful ways to navigate the ocean depths.

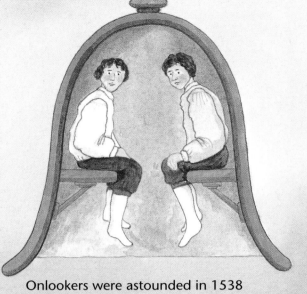

Onlookers were astounded in 1538 when two Greeks crawled into a diving bell, submerged for 20 minutes and then resurfaced unharmed. How did the bell work? Try "The Diving Glass" to find out.

In 1776 American inventor and mechanic David Bushnell built a submarine called the *Turtle*. It looked like two turtle shells attached belly to belly and was barely large enough to fit one person. The driver sat upright, peering out of the portholes at eye level, and hand-cranked the propellors to make the sub move.

The first vessel used to descend deep into the ocean was a bathysphere designed by naturalist William Beebe. His ball-shaped vessel had no propellors and just hung in the water on a heavy steel cable tethered to the support ship. A second cable carried electricity for light and a telephone connection to the surface. Divers breathed from cylinders of air stored inside the bathysphere. In 1934, Beebe took his invention to a record depth of 923 m (3028 feet). He became the first person to see and photograph deep-sea organisms. Turn to page 68 to see some of the creatures he might have found.

Modern submarines and submersibles can remain underwater for a long time and many don't require a cable from a surface ship. They are equipped with photographic equipment, collecting arms, sampling devices and other equipment for underwater research.

Unmanned submersibles called ROVs (Remotely Operated Vehicles) are used to film and collect deep-sea animals. They are operated by a pilot in a research ship at the surface.

The diving glass

Turn an ordinary drinking glass into a diving bell.

1. Try to put your glass into a sink full of water without getting the inside of the glass wet. Impossible, you say?

2. Dry off your glass and try this. Hold the open end of the glass straight over the surface of the water and plunge it into the water. The air inside the glass will be trapped there and no water will be able to enter.

3. Don't believe it? Put a crumpled-up paper towel in the bottom of the glass and try it again. Did the paper towel get wet?

Early diving bells worked the same way. The air trapped inside the bell kept water out. Divers breathed the stored air. But diving bells could be dangerous. Tip the glass slightly while it is submerged and you'll see why.

Canadian engineers have developed the "Newtsuit," a flexible, one-person submarine. This hard suit allows divers to work independently, without attachment to the surface, as deep as 305 m (1000 feet). This suit is used in construction and research projects.

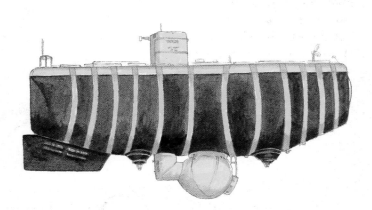

In 1960, Dr. Jacques Picard and U.S. Navy lieutenant Don Walsh climbed into a bathyscaphe called the *Trieste I* and descended 10 912 m (35 800 feet) into the Mariana Trench, one of the deepest known places in the ocean. Their record for the world's deepest dive still holds today.

Deep-sea wonders

Living in the dark and the cold requires special equipment. Deep-sea fish have what they need built in.

DARK-BUSTERS

Many deep-sea creatures can light up. Some grow luminescent (light-giving) bacteria in pouches, called photophores. This ability to make light is called bioluminescence. Deep-sea creatures use their ability to bioluminesce in a variety of ways.

Lanternfish migrate at night to the upper ocean to feed on zooplankton. An ordinary fish would be silhouetted against the moonlit surface of the upper waters, making it easy prey for predators. Not the lantern-fish. By lighting up photophores along the bottom of its body, it seems to disappear in the moonlit water. Many other deep-sea fish also use this "counterlighting" as camouflage.

Some **deep-sea jellyfish** trail lighted tentacles behind them. If threatened, they can turn off their body lights and drop off their glowing tentacles. The predator dives for the tentacles and the jellyfish escapes.

SEEING IN THE DARK

Fish that live in the twilight zone often have very large eyes relative to their body size. Others have special lenses that can detect bioluminescence or make use of the small amount of light in the depths.

Some **hatchetfish** have eyes that point upwards to scan the waters above them for zooplankton. Their eyes act like telescopes and can focus up close or far away.

Some **deep-sea squid** have one eye that is much larger than the other. Some scientists think that they must swim with their small eye looking down and their large eye looking up. By doing so, the large eye could gather the little bit of light that comes from the surface, while the smaller

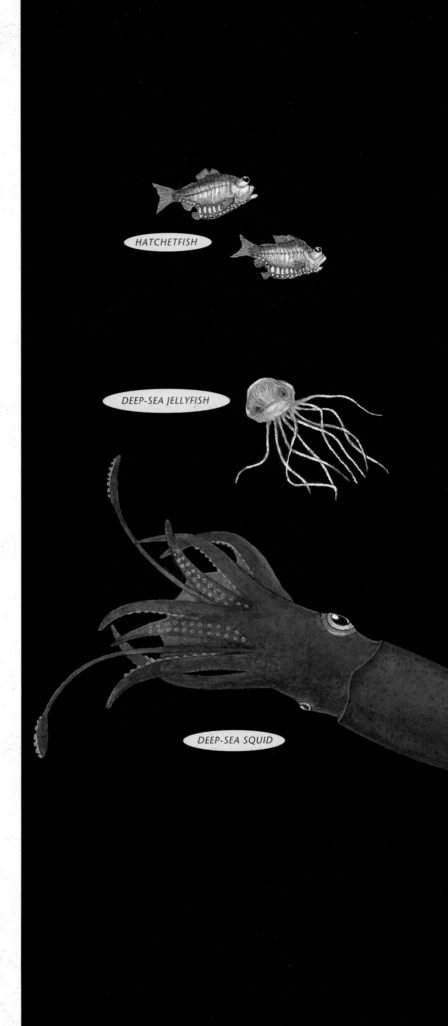

HATCHETFISH

DEEP-SEA JELLYFISH

DEEP-SEA SQUID

LANTERNFISH

VIPERFISH

ANGLERFISH

DEEP-SEA ARROW-WORMS

eye could see light from the photophores of other squid or fish.

Animals that dwell in the darkness of the deep sea usually have very small eyes or none at all. No eyes are necessary where there is no light. Instead of sight they rely on other senses, such as smell.

FINDING FOOD

Most deep-sea fish discovered so far are quite small, so they don't need much food. This helps them survive in their food-scarce habitat. To get whatever food there is, some creatures have come up with amazing fishing methods.

The **viperfish's** fangs are so large it can't close its mouth. It swims with its jaws wide open, so wide it can swallow prey several times larger than itself. To make sure there are no slip-ups, its teeth curve backwards – squiggling prey, once caught, are trapped.

The **anglerfish** dangles a lighted lure in front of its mouth to attract prey. To cope with extra-big meals, anglerfish and other deep-sea fish have stretchy stomachs.

HUNTING FOR A MATE

Finding a mate can be difficult in the dark. Some animals recognize potential mates by their unique pattern of photophores. Others have a well-developed sense of smell. Anglerfish are super-sniffers. Once a male, which is tiny in comparison to the female, finds a female by scent, he bites into her side and permanently attaches himself as a parasite. The parasitic male relies on the female for food. His main function is for reproduction.

Other animals, such as **deep-sea arrow-worms**, have eliminated the need for a partner to mate with by becoming both male and female. These animals can make both eggs and sperm and, if necessary, can fertilize themselves.

Eat or be eaten

The ocean is a never-ending smorgasbord for the creatures living there. Almost everything in the ocean, whether it is large or small, living or dead, is used as food. The relationship between the eaters and the eaten (predators and prey) is called a food chain. Here is a typical food chain:

The **sun** provides energy and is the powerhouse that drives food chains.

Phytoplankton, the tiny plants of the sea, turn the sun's energy into food for themselves.

Zooplankton, the floating animals of the sea, eat the phytoplankton.

Smaller fish, such as **anchovies** or **herring**, eat the zooplankton.

Larger fish, such as **salmon**, eat the smaller fish.

At the end of the chain a top predator, such as a **killer whale**, eats the larger fish.

Where do you fit in?

Are you part of an ocean food chain? Try drawing a marine food chain that includes you and a tuna sandwich.

Chain or web?

Most animals don't eat just one type of food. When you add variety, the food chain looks more like a food web.

The animals get larger as you move through the chain. Even dead plants and animals play an important role in ocean food chains. Scavengers such as crabs and bacteria eat the dead plants and animals and return the nutrients back to the sea to be used again.

If one link in the food chain is damaged or lost, the whole chain must adjust. But sometimes a broken link has devastating consequences. Some plants or animals lose their main source of food. To survive, they must adapt and find new food. Others lose their main predator. Without a predator to keep their numbers down, their population explodes and many go hungry.

Food chains can be threatened by pollution, overfishing and other disturbances. On the Pacific coast of North America, the results were dramatic when the kelp-sea urchin-sea otter food chain was disrupted. Usually, sea otters eat the sea urchins, which eat kelp. The otters kept the urchin population in check. Everything changed when sea otters were hunted almost to extinction in the mid 1700s. There was an explosion in the sea urchin population. Huge numbers of urchins moved like an army through kelp forests, devouring them as they went. The areas left behind were called urchin barrens. They looked like marine moonscapes. Instead of kelp, there was a blanket of sea urchins. The kelp forests – important habitats to many sea animals – were wiped out.

Today, sea otters are protected and there are thriving kelp forests once again.

Sea otters (above) eat **sea urchins** (left), which eat **kelp** (below).

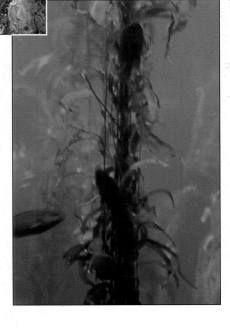

Ocean diners

To survive, all animals must eat. Some eat plants and are called herbivores. Others eat animals and are called carnivores. Still others eat both plants and animals and are called omnivores. Are you a herbivore, a carnivore or an omnivore?

Regardless of what they eat, ocean animals have developed special ways to feed on their favourite foods.

Imagine chewing on tough, rubbery kelp all day. Your jaws would get pretty tired. But that doesn't stop a **sea urchin**. Kelp is one of its favourite foods. Although a sea urchin has only five teeth in its circular mouth, its jaws are superstrong, with 40 bones and 60 muscles. ►

▲ **Jellyfish**, sea anemones, corals and their relatives have a hidden weapon in their tentacles – stinging cells called nematocysts. Inside each nematocyst is a long, coiled thread that is triggered by touch. The threads shoot out like a harpoon and barbs grab onto the prey. Sometimes poison is injected. Then the predator drags its victim into its body and begins to eat.

▲ **Marine tube worms** have long, delicate feeding tentacles that stick out the top of their tube. These filters trap any food drifting by and carry it down to the worm's mouth. Many other animals are filter feeders, too. Try "Be a Filter Feeder" to see how filters capture food.

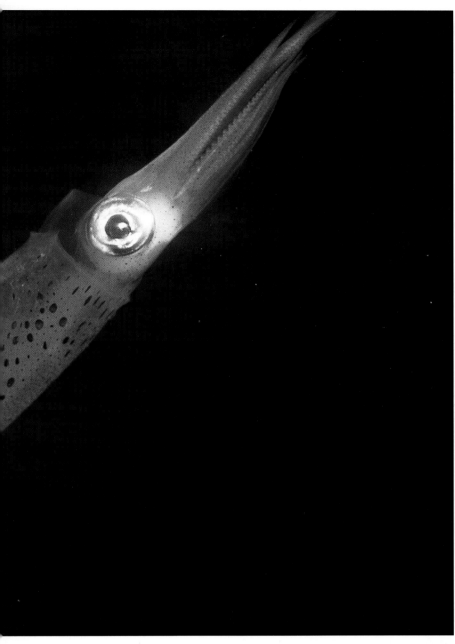

▲ A **squid** uses jet propulsion to dart after its prey, which it grabs with its tentacles. A quick bite with its sharp beaklike mouth kills the prey, and the squid chomps it down.

▲ Where would we be without garbage collectors? The **California sea cucumber** moves along the ocean floor like a mini-marine vacuum cleaner, eating mud and sand and digesting any dead plant or animal matter in it.

Be a filter feeder

Many marine creatures, including some whales, filter food out of the water. Their filters work like a sieve – the water passes through the sieve and the food stays behind. Try it and see for yourself.

You'll need:
a shallow pan of water
ground pepper
a comb (with teeth fairly close together)

1. Sprinkle pepper grains on the surface of the water. Run your finger through the pepper. How much pepper did you capture?

2. Now take a sweep through the pepper with the comb. Compare how much pepper you captured using the two methods.

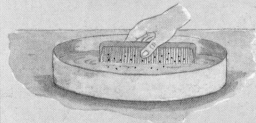

The comb acts like the filter-feeding equipment of marine creatures. Filter feeders use their filters in different ways. Barnacles wave their filters in the water and can swivel them to meet the food-carrying currents. Filter-feeding fish simply swim with their mouths open, capturing food in special gill rakers.

Attack and defence

When animals aren't eating, they are trying to avoid being eaten. Shells, spines, camouflage, toxins and ink are some of the weapons animals use to fend off predators.

◄ Shells are fortresses for some sea creatures. This **whelk** has a trapdoor, called an operculum, attached to its foot. When the operculum is pulled up into the shell, the whelk's enemies can't get at the soft, fleshy body inside.

▲ This **hermit crab** takes over the empty shells of dead snails. It has to, otherwise its soft abdomen would make it easy prey. As the hermit crab grows, it must find larger and larger shells.

◄ If the **sunflower star**'s arm is grabbed by a predator, it can drop off the arm and scuttle away. Over time, the sunflower star will grow a new arm. Other animals, such as brittle stars, sea cucumbers and some crabs, can also drop off parts of their bodies.

Nudibranchs are tiny, brightly coloured sea slugs that don't look particularly harmful. But those beautiful bright colours are a warning to predators – don't touch! Why? For one thing, nudibranchs taste awful. For another, some nudibranchs borrow weapons from other animals. They can eat anemones and their cousins, stinging cells and all, without getting stung themselves. Then they use the stinging cells for their own defence. ▶

The **octopus** is a master of disguises. It can change its skin colour and texture instantly to blend in with the changing background as it moves through the water. And it can leave a "smoke-screen" of ink behind if a predator gets too close. The ink hides the octopus's escape route. ▼

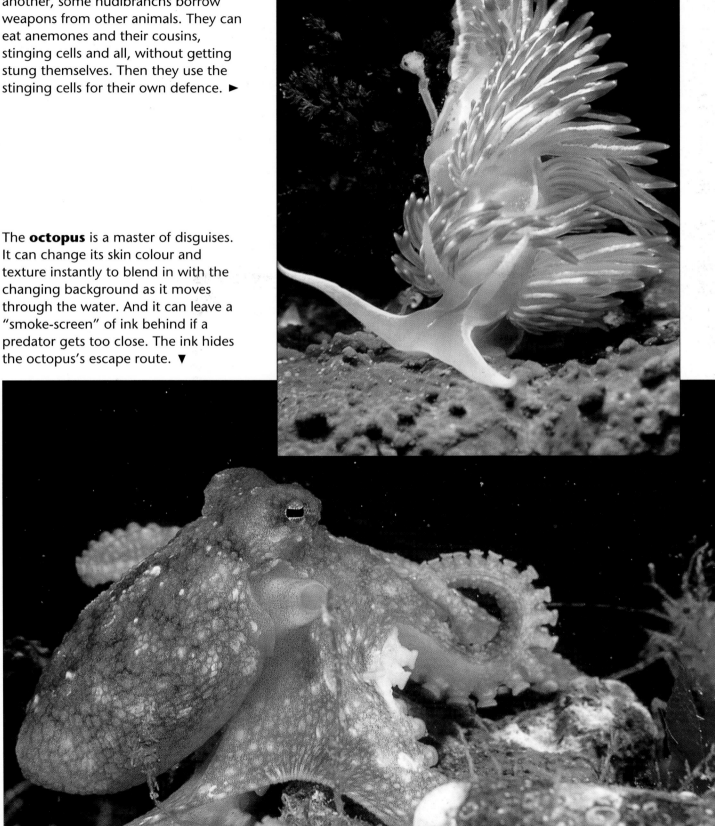

Ocean alert!

It's a scorching hot day and you feel like a dip in the ocean. But when you arrive at the beach, you find this sign: Beach Unsafe for Swimming. The lifeguard tells you that sewage dumped nearby has polluted the beach.

We have used the ocean as a garbage dump for centuries. Sewage, toxic wastes, nuclear wastes, fertilizers, pesticides, oil and garbage have been dumped into the ocean. Pollution that prevents you from having a cool swim on a hot day is a nuisance – for the animals and plants that live in the ocean, it can be a disaster. Pollution can disrupt marine food chains. Imagine what would happen in the food chain on page 70 if all of the fish died because of pollution. Would the killer whales have anything to eat? Try the experiments on the next page to see how pollution affects marine life.

What can you do to help?

- *Educate yourself, your friends and your family about the ocean. When you understand something, you tend to take better care of it.*

- *Avoid buying seashells or other gift items made from sea creatures. Collect only those shells you are lucky enough to find on the beach.*

- *Take part in beach clean-up campaigns.*

- *Dispose of garbage in a safe and environmentally friendly way. Don't dump garbage in the ocean or any body of water. Take your garbage home with you.*

- *Even if you don't live near the ocean, monitor how your local lakes and rivers are being treated. Remember: all water eventually reaches the ocean.*

Oil pollution

News reports about oil spills, often show pictures of oil-soaked birds struggling to stay alive. Why is oil so damaging? Try this to find out.

You'll need:
a feather from a feather pillow or quilt
vegetable oil

1. Dip the feather in water and look at it closely. Use a magnifying glass if you have one. Dry the feather.

2. Dip the feather in the vegetable oil and have another look. How did the feather change?

Birds and marine mammals such as sea otters keep warm by trapping air in the soft, downy feathers or fur next to their skin. These air pockets warm up and keep the animal warm. Oil sticks feathers or fur together. The air spaces collapse and can't hold in body heat.

Plastic pollution

Turtles mistake plastic bags for jellyfish and eat them. Birds and fish get caught in plastic six-pack rings. And birds and mammals get fouled in discarded fishing lines and nets. What is it like to get tangled up in plastic? Try this and see.

1. Place a thick rubber band around your hand as shown.

2. Try to remove the rubber band without using your teeth or other hand or by rubbing it against your body.

If an animal gets caught in a six-pack ring, it may starve, strangle or suffocate. Dispose of plastic garbage, on land, in a garbage can.

Answers

Corals, page 38:

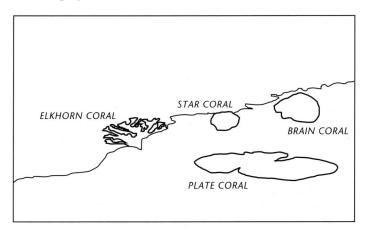

STAR CORAL

ELKHORN CORAL

BRAIN CORAL

PLATE CORAL

Who's who, page 44:
1A, 2D, 3B, 4E, 5C.

Body shape: A habitat clue, page 48:
sole, sandy bottom
angelfish, coral
pipefish, eelgrass
wolf eel, rock crevice

Glossary

abdomen: the rear part of the body of a crab or other arthropod

arthropod: a group of animals with hard jointed exterior skeletons instead of bones. Includes crabs, shrimps and insects.

bacteria: simple, one-celled organisms that help decay (break down) plant and animal tissue. This decay makes nutrients available to other organisms.

camouflage: colouring or markings on an animal's body that help it blend in with its surroundings and escape detection by predators

condense: to change from a gas to a liquid. Warm air condenses on a cool window to form water droplets.

dehydrated: dried out due to loss of water or moisture

evaporate: to change from a liquid to a gas

gills: organs used by fish and many water-dwelling animals to take oxygen from water

gravity: the force of attraction that causes things to fall towards the centre of the Earth

intertidal: the part of seashore between the high tide and low tide levels

kelp: large brown seaweed

magma: hot fluid rock beneath the Earth's crust. Magma turns to rock when it hardens.

mucus: a slimy secretion

operculum: hard plate that covers the opening of snails' shells and some tubeworms' tubes

parasite: an animal or plant that lives on or in another living thing and obtains nutrition from its host

plankton: organisms that drift or float with the currents

predator: an animal that captures and eats another animal

prey: an animal captured for food by another animal

scavenger: an animal that feeds on dead or decaying matter

tentacles: slender, flexible appendages used for feeding, defence and/or respiration

Index